# A Guide to Maintaining a Sound Economy

## Madeline Chambers

iUniverse, Inc.
Bloomington

# A Guide to Maintaining a Sound Economy

iUniverse books may be ordered through booksellers or by contacting:

iUniverse
1663 Liberty Drive
Bloomington, IN 47403
www.iuniverse.com
1-800-Authors (1-800-288-4677)

ISBN: 978-1-4502-8110-2 (sc)
ISBN: 978-1-4502-8111-9 (ebook)

Printed in the United States of America

iUniverse rev. date: 1/13/2011

This book is dedicated to honest, hard working, wise and ethical people everywhere, and to my mother, who, like me, recognize that good faith is part of fairness, in a world of increased global dependence and the increased need for good faith, for a sustainable and healthy economy…

It was J.R.R. Tolkien who said-

*"All that is gold does not glitter,*
*Not all those who wander are lost..."*

About the author: Madeline Chambers is a Social Political Scientist mentality, and Realist, who has a background in business as a professional Accountant and Consultant in Silicon Valley, and whose education includes a degree in Liberal Studies with Political Science and Business Administration studies also completed. She is currently attempting to pursue a second degree in the same academic category of learning, and following interests in technical and business special course work toward a greater specialization, in a business world which has become increasingly technical.

Madeline, who was born and raised in California, has also studied: American, European and World History; Anthropology; Psychology; and completed studies in Business Law; Case Law as well as Investigation; Insurance and Code and Ethics Pre-licensing; Religious studies; Theology; Human Resources; Economics and Marketing; Biology; Greek; Latin; Italian; and Hebrew Languages and literature studies, and the Classics of Literature, as well as Philosophy as minor concentrations in her studies, in various years of her studies, over the course of a span of 20 years of total adult education and work experience in Silicon Valley, in Northern California.

A former honors student scholar, Madeline has been an unpublished writer for 15 years, of children's stories, clinical Psychology and Sociology studies, among entrepreneurial pursuits, until she became sufficiently inspired, and had time to complete this book.

In discussion with associates in the business world and among law and education scholars, her book is viewed as "timely" and "insightful", concerning business practices, government and economics, in the present modern global economy.

General and specific education, the reflection upon it, social statistics, analysis of business markets, numerous documentaries, radio broadcasts, programs and broadcasts on C-span, a few BBC and a number of Wall Street Journal broadcasts, which have shaped and contributed

to the total completion of this informative reporting of facts, and commentary style, quick-read book.

This book is an attempt to provide the reader with an explanation of how business and economic structure works, with reference to business examples and the analysis of economic structure and business practice, the financial markets description of recent corrected activities of the SEC, Treasury and Financial and business sectors in America, regulation, and what has taken place in our modern and present Economy in America, its security, with statistics references and some direct quotes from governing and business professional authorities of great experience and wisdom, with some commentary concerning the business experience studied as well as my own experience, the history of America references, Senators and leaders, in business practice reviewed, and application of principles related to business experience and economics from experience in the working world, including my own...

First things first: Central to the understanding of life, business in general, the Economy, and good governance, one needs to understand that fundamental Constitutional provisions were written down, for all time, in the *Constitution of the United States of America*, and *The Declaration of Independence, for the benefit* of all citizens in *any* society, certainly after the *creation* of Civil Rights, through the Civil War from 1861-1865, and during the time of the leadership of President Lincoln, in our Nation's history, whose leadership did follow the *Declaration of Independence*, of 1776. One needs to have a fundamental understanding of Economics as well. One needs albeit to understand the 7 fundamental principles that are necessary to watch carefully, involved in *sustaining a balanced* Economy, let alone an *out-of-control* Economy we have recently begun to recover from, *in just 18 months of new hope, in a brand new Washington, D.C., White House administration which was bequeathed a bankrupted Economy, hitherto, in a reeling* America, under the Bush Administration. There are 7 principles to keep in mind, for those who wish to understand how to balance the Economy and to keep it that way, which is simpler than you may think. First of all, in the world, as the cost of living is affected by the rise in prices, the best thing that can be done to keep the economy stable, first of all, is, as economists agree in general statistics and research, to keep stable, wages and retail prices. Wages that can as closely as possible, match the cost of living, when the ups and downs of the market hit, and inflation starts to become a problem, are vital. Many people may know this but not be able to articulate it; however they intrinsically know it as they pay attention to facts and watch their pennies. They too understand that as Lincoln stated: "a penny saved, is a penny earned". Power without accountability, means nothing. That was always true in history, and smart people know this, too. It was not just President James Madison who knew and spoke of this, in America's history.

Abraham Lincoln printed money when he could not afford to borrow to go to war, back at the time of the Confederacy and Civil War. So, he printed money, yet, he had to exercise *restraint* so that he did not print too much, *so that inflation would not get out of control and destroy the economy.* Had Lincoln printed too much money for that smaller economy and population, back then, compared to our economy and population today, he might have created too much inflation by doing so. As it was, he created treasury bills and saved the Nation, back then, creating the "*greenback*" with green ink and preserving it and our future economies. Banks don't like the idea of printing money because they cannot get from the printed money, the return they would want as when money that is backed by the Treasury is already part of the economic system, so governance either chooses to print more money and to charge more or higher taxes, or in a crisis, to borrow and spend. Since the money system in America and borrowing had become a spending problem under the Bush administration which created large deficits, the next administration had to act quickly to ensure value in the money system, which the previous administration had devalued by over-borrowing. Thus, *hard earned money* being put into the treasury to back up debt, incurred by the choices of the Nation's wealthiest citizens and the Bush administration, which those who enjoy ease at the top of the pyramid, don't feel the pain, and since printing money would be too dangerous for such a large deficit problem, due to such a large deficit and population, it was too risky in our modern times, essentially to do what Lincoln did, back when he did in that economy, so long ago, especially, in short order, in this modern, out- of -control economy...

And, as a rule in life, before any journey can be started, people must have sufficient hope to begin it...

# The Principle to Maintaining Good or Sound Economics Involves Sound Business Practice and Proper Regulation:

The principle to maintaining sound economics or fiscal responsibility and economic balance, is to earn wisely and to save prudently, to educate citizens to do so, *to create and foster a balanced and fair economy, in good faith*, (do we recall what '*good faith*' used to be?), and never to spend more than you need to, in living conservatively, saving for a rainy day, and making do without living beyond one's means, much less a governments' means, and to be able to negotiate fairly for what one *truly needs*, so that *all conservators or holders* of the *greenback* or *dollar* are indeed *Just*, given one's income, in good faith business, generating *true* equal opportunity, and not *merely* the *appearance* of it, which is part of an 'unfit' economy—and, what *appears to be job growth, but in fact is not, which America found out was inspired by the business practices of the Bush administration in its tax and spend policies, before consideration of health and well-being became an even greater issue for Democrats to solve, along with the looming deficit created by the business practices of the Bush administration. The Democrats, suddenly locked out for attending to the very real needs of the people who need an equal share in prosperity, within American shores.*

What, therefore is also essential to running *good* business and *maintaining a balance in the economy,* is paying on one's debts and being able to see clearly to doing so, and discouraging out-of-control spending, which is critical to keeping inflation low, controlling out-of-control deregulated mass business, reducing scams in an economy and having good and fair competition in any society, let alone opportunities and proper accountability in business and governance. Next, what maintains a sound economy is to tax successful business, to prepare for the security of the Nation, which is just *wise* business. To not overtax specifically volatile sectors of people and business, is crucial, as we have seen, and concerning big business, which hesitates to govern itself when it comes to oil spills or fair dealings, foreign markets and personal, as well as global accountability, creates crisis in our Nation. All we have to do is watch the News. C-Span has been extremely informative in the last two years, in numerous non-moderated Senate Hearings, and other meetings and socio-political events and business association programs, for those who seek continually to educate themselves, daily.

The way people live is not an equation, but it certainly *becomes one over time.* The ingredients for success are found in the ways people save and wisely spend their money and manage business. It is a misnomer and incorrect to say that only spending is an issue in any economy, regarding the need to set up protections for people who have lower wages in a society where people need consumer protections and low cost, moderate and continually monitored healthcare, as well as other necessary regulations in business, to keep the public safe in high economic growth cycles, particularly, and to maximize economic productivity and sufficiency. The rich never feel the need for low cost healthcare, moderate healthcare it seems, or much regulation, as they want to be free to generate profits, with little to no accountability, as you will see, later in this text. The same is true of wages in general: The rich seem to feel little need to adjust them. In the last eight years particularly, America has witnessed this phenomenon most profoundly. Those who pay the wages and live comfortably are less sensitive to how far those wages go, in the same economy, as they are becoming rich, typically… as we have seen…

*So, in a free country, concerning the issue of freedom, are we to believe, that the modern Nation's previous American Government Administration's view, of business becoming based upon who is "lucky" enough to get to freedom first, or to get there any way they can, is not outdated in many significant ways? …*

Therefore, how business can be *fairly regulated to serve all peoples' interests unto a fair, and balanced system that serves all people, is, in a balanced economy,* much more important to address, and more so in an out- of -control economy, *concerning constantly evaluating what is constitutional, in today's economy and world, and attending to and amending it. THAT is what the Constitution provides for: How to practice wise business and economic balance as well as to maintain justice.* THAT is a hard and very necessary principle to maintain, as Lincoln himself said in his time, concerning saving the people and governing in *his* time: "you can please some of the people some of the time, but you cannot please all of the people all of the time", which is not a subject of pundit rhetoric, by the way. This simply means that in order to run a Nation and not to keep everyone on a plantation, there needs to be proper taxation upon those who do business along with everyone else in a *shared Nation* in which resources are shrinking, in today's world, and where the tax burden upon the middleclass has recently been just too burdensome not to be shared with the privileged who enjoy a life of ease, by comparison.

Essentially, and existentially, in business and concerning Economics, you must weigh economic "intrinsic costs" versus "extrinsic costs", or economic "opportunity costs", to improve any economy, while weighing the long term interests of a sustainable economy and peoples' needs. Peoples' needs and the numbers of the needy simply outweigh the *desires* of special interests, in a *balanced* economy, where big business has a huge margin of capital compared to those who have less or little… *even more pronounced is the need for shared burden in an out-*

*of-control economy,* such as we have been experiencing recently, if you check the employment statistics and import export status, concerning the G20 summit and the WTO: World Trade Organization, as well as small business recovery which overall seems not to have recovered just yet, across America if you are watching... But I will talk more about that later in the text...

In other words, what is a modicum amount of tax upon the wealthy, comparatively speaking, compared to those who struggle to pay taxes, is a just use of law and the Constitution, in the notion of the constitutional law clause, which deals with the "*laying and collecting of taxes*" upon business, *as we as a Nation are finding is now on the table, and coming due, after the Bush tax breaks for the wealthiest Americans, which continued for at least, eight years, which led to the current status of this present economy.* This therefore, does not mean that the interests of those at the disadvantage cannot be served in some ways in a balanced economy, it means simply, that an advantaged society has the Constitutional *Responsibility* and *Obligation* to make the necessary provisions to *preserve the rights* and *interests* of those at the greater disadvantage, along with all others, especially if the needy are in such large numbers or, disproportionately in the *majority, as the Constitution makes provision for justice in the deeds of men in business, ever since slavery was abolished by President Lincoln.* In a *well managed* economy and its populace, there must be *proper business protections* applied to business, regularly, with proper legislation, and *proper taxation, for all, in business, to maintain a safe and balanced economy and society, as we are now just beginning to see emerge after only 18 months of the brand new Administration which is currently in place, who are under more scrutiny than the Bush Administration of eight years, which led us into to this crisis.*

Taxation, presently, must be distributed as well, among those who must make provision for the *security* of a Nation, to show restraint, where a high margin of adequate wealth in a group or population of higher income bracketed individuals, contribute to shared responsibility of taxes, so as not to leave the tax burden disproportionately upon smaller, struggling groups of Americans among the masses, who struggle for the need of *adequate economic freedom and relief*, which was clearly defined, finally for the Nation as a whole, in the $787 Billion Dollar Bail Out, full blown Financial crisis. There is no substitute for *proper governance in business*. The only way that proper governance can be performed, is not through ignoring, as stated by responsible authorities, but rather through legislation and safeguards to continually monitor and check the activities of those in places of financial responsibility, as we witnessed as a Nation in the $787 Billion Dollar Bail Out Hearings, in the last few months, in those non-moderated Hearing floor broadcasts of just the Senators on C-Span. Since President Madison did say regarding power: "Absolute power corrupts absolutely", one has to examine who has the *power* in any society, and the *responsibility* to manage responsibly, in the face of economic strain and change, in a Nation.

Responsibility is *shared by big business corporate interest* and government, in taxes, and taxation should be equally shared by big business and corporations, along with the small business man, because the Constitution and its provisions, and business work hand in hand, and the laws therefore legislated by the Constitution and its forefathers, if you read *The Constitution of the United States of America* which made provision for taxes to be paid by all persons in business so that the *problem of totalitarian oligarchies* would not be repeated in America, which is at the very root of America's origin. Americans had come from such Colonial oppression originally. Eventually, slavery was seen as bestial and abolished at the time of the Civil War of 1861-1865 under President Lincoln following the Emancipation Proclamation at Gettysburg.

Since power is money, one must examine politically, which constituent base has the greater access to that power, in any group, who the constituencies are, and what they stand to gain, because life is also essentially, political as well as monetary in nature, (although those who are politically and financially powerful, often seem to play down their political status and hope you will ignore them and their knowledge, in the modern political arena). President Hoover said: "The worst thing about Capitalism is the Capitalist". Groups would not exist to protect interests of those at a disadvantage, if they were not *necessary*. So, the *right to assemble* and to *vote* is *critical*, as is the voice of the people, and regulation. Basic Economics teaches a few principles if you check Economics textbooks and research online. (These terms or nomenclature is commonly used):

What produces a *balance* in any economy is, first: Avoiding inflation:

Economists tend to agree as a rule about what creates inflation. For instance:

Demand which sets off inflation is thought of by economists to be the cause of inflation—that is, demand which causes inflation by raising costs and prices. But people know it is people who raise prices intentionally, in the *supply and demand* chain and flow of goods and services in an open free market of business enterprise.

# Strategies for Maintaining a Sound Economy and the Seven Principles to Watch in Maintaining the Balance of a Sound Domestic and Foreign Economy:

Strategies for Sound business practice and the maintenance of a sound economic structure, now and well into the future, concerning the economic *positive opportunity curve* of social interest, involve specific actions to be taken to preserve the stability of *any economy*, which includes the modern costs of opportunity in doing business in today's economy and the follow-up reports from modern divergence statistics at present, which give indicators as to what will engender the best overall business practices and strategies for governance in the modern world economy, of present and future political interest, now and well into the future, which requires constant care and attention to the financial and business machine, determined recently by Senators in Hearings held in our Nation's capital city and broadcasted on C-span. All business sectors, both Public and Private, depend upon profits and revenues that demand *honest* and *transparent* sustainability for the survival of *all* citizens or people in one global economy, according to Senators from Congress and Senate, and Hearings, viewed on C-Span.

This book is an attempt to provide the reader with an explanation of how business and economic structure works, with reference to business examples and the analysis of economic structure and business practice, the financial markets description of recent corrected activities of the SEC, Treasury and Financial and business sectors in America, regulation, and what has taken place in our modern and present Economy, in America, its security, with statistics references and some direct quotes from governing and business professional authorities of great experience and wisdom, with some commentary concerning the business experience studied as well as my own experience, some history of America references, business practice and application of principles related to business experience and economics from experience in the working world, including my own... There are seven conditions that take place in an economy and principles involved in maintaining a sound economy, which I will mention in detail later, after providing information and background on an unregulated economy and a shifting economic curve, which in part, occurs due to some basic business practices. Government regulation will be addressed as well.

This all started happening in the 1980's, about thirty years or so ago... Life started to get out of control in the Nation we call America. The world was changing, that is, undergoing its own revolution, and deregulation was becoming a challenge in business, to the extent that people wanted to make large amounts of money, in an unregulated economy. As time passed, starting with the Reagan era, continuing right on through, and up into the 1990's, getting more challenging and escalating into the year 2000, with the next president George Herbert Walker Bush, where more and more deregulation for business growth was the primary interest and goal to in essence provide as well, access to good jobs, a good living, which did for some citizens, while other citizens served well in business and essentially were asked to sacrifice access to higher quality of living and education, in some cases, and, in some cases, to put their futures on hold for the Economic Revolution. Education has long been hailed the bastion of hope and opportunity in America, where service leads to opportunities for those who serve and work harder, or at least, it used to be so in America, where people were rewarded for their hard work and contributions to American business. Gradually, less then acceptable apologies were doled out, in place of the progress and the equal opportunities for the hardest working, literate Americans, and offers no longer extended to some harder working literate Americans, while no amendments were made during the 1990's, due to the emergence of a lifestyle which leaned toward privilege and away from fundamental business opportunity, equity, fairness, good faith, sound economic practice, and equality for far too many Americans. Later, following the administration of Herbert Walker Bush, George Walker Bush took over the surplus that President Clinton created, and plunged our economy into a near Great Depression. This happened gradually. Some aware citizens warned people over and over, seeking legal authorities regarding questionable business practices, and informing businesses what could happen to them in terms of lost revenues and reputation, in the local media, before 1990, should they continue their practices, to find they incurred what was projected for their bottom line and their respective reputations, regarding their business practice, as many of us, were sent across the landscape of the modern business Manifest Destiny syndrome of myriad such business practices, and then, the "changing of the guard" of power, to continue the modern Manifest Destiny method of deregulation in pursuit of rich revenues, quick schemes and quick business, less attention to detail, in data and management, and the costs, which people who manage with clarity realized could not sustain such practices over time, only to watch a gradual decline of business, and more changes in business practice, and not surprisingly, the bottom line, as predicted, due to a decline in business regulation, governance, and concern in the Private and Public sectors. I had the chance to intern at a Civil, Criminal and Probate legal office among other, and manufacturing opportunities, Hi-Tech and Biotech as well as Defense, (before Defense was legislated toward closures, during a business cycle of the Economy), and consulting in Accountancy practice in Silicon Valley, some twenty years before the full blown American Markets Financial crisis hit, to weather the effects of deregulation and work with the business standards at that time, having audited business and some which were indeed more interested in making money than doing business in a manner which was good for their longevity, or the staff in general, purely economically speaking, as a professional Accountant and Consultant. There were those who were loyal in business and ignored for their good service, and good faith, being told they were good and above average, praised for their service and being told they were the outstanding, not properly remunerated, in some cases, who had been screened out to be hired into service for the more wisely screened, at the higher level of service, out of hundreds of candidates for employee service loyalty. I was one of them- I survived. I never liked controversy but often had to speak addressing it, as well as inequality and concerning integrity. Leaving others to account for the responsibility of executives is less than professional, if for no other reason, than doing business demands good faith, concerning efficiency and true professionalism, which also includes accountability and maintaining proper records as well as efficiency as professionals do. Those who earn the right to serve also earn the right to speak freely in working for American prosperity, which is the good faith good citizens *create* with their *good service*, which America seemed to forget over time just a bit, with the Dot Com craze whose bubble burst right about the year 2000 or 2001 I think, which was tell-tale of how incentivizing the profit motive finally became an issue, in Silicon Valley. It is wise to build business and to keep it local and to reinvest in one's infrastructure for true prosperity, and its individual investments, carefully, as Europe has done, increasing the value of its Euros, as opposed to lowering the value of the dollar, leading to crisis, obviously, whenever and wherever that occurs, obviously.

Everyone seemed to become dizzy in the economy, seeking the wealth-generating incentive centered outcomes, and many became tired, overworked and even traumatized with the manners and modes of business and the modus operandi of so many wealth-dazzled seekers who sought riches during those times, which seemed contrary to the brick- by-brick building strategy of the Realist American thinkers and planners who preferred efficiency and avoidance of systems failures due to inattention to detail, then systems failure analysis, which all too often came too late and was too costly, as regards oversight, concerning inefficient compliance. As a result, the financial sector felt they could get away with more, since inattention to detail in governance was the rule and not the exception. This led to the crisis of the $787 billion dollar bail out. Politicians tend to think in election and legislative policy time frames, while business for the businessman is ongoing and works in different time lines than government, which may be an insight into why the infrastructure situation became what it did. However, some may be tempted to justify what business and government did, which is no justification in light of understood standards of proper business conduct in a Nation and how they ought to conduct themselves. *We, the educated, do understand this, well.* Those with the *greater access* have the *greater responsibility* in any Nation or Country. This is precisely why slaves were freed and encouraged toward independence by President Lincoln.

In the years of 1990 to 2006, the downward spiral of *outsourcing* and businesses *trying to encourage business with China* accounts and account making, in many fields, (for those of us who had become consultants in Silicon Valley and were aware of this trend), that is, of America gaining China accounts and outsourcing which was escalating in American business practice and American business management style, while imports and exports went largely it seemed to me, unchecked in our economy, as the fascination with China and the East, its medicinal appeal, manufacturing and the practice of meditation from the far East and business prospects, began to charm the West. A sizable Indian population began its migration to the United States and many settled near where I live, in sunny California, in the Bay Area, to be precise, in towns nearby and near my city. Education became an issue as America seemed disproportionately "differentially" educated, particularly in Math and Science, and still is somewhat less educated in some areas, compared to European and some Indian suburb dwellers I know and have known, with Visas who travel to the U.S. and relocate here, as the U.S. has an educational rating in Math and Science today, Nationally, statistically, of 17th; compared to that of Finland, and 50th, globally, in education, institutionally, which is considered low, globally, considering its wealth, and the opportunities for those of us who had to work harder in some cases, but whose performance was much higher than average, and professional, in keeping pace with the highly educated professionals, with the excuse that we were "overqualified" or not yet properly degreed, when seeking proper advancement toward and more secure financial future, which has been the right of every hard-working citizen, regardless of gender, race or background, when we were super conscientious harder-working, seeking higher equal opportunities in business and education, being significantly qualified, extremely literate and articulate, even compared to others with their comparatively more easily procured degrees and help from family, as well, as interviewers would make plain. (Those from a life of comparative ease were not disadvantaged and could spend fulltime in school, to start, without having to work and earn the privilege of attending fulltime education, and whose parents were not as poor, by comparison), while we picked up ourselves by our bootstraps and did most of the infrastructure work efficiently, often, in comparison, without complaint, be it cheerfully, which the ease of the lives of the privileged, with all due respect, many of us did not have, and were not given equal access to jobs and careers in what was perceivably a biased society which many of we career professionals talked about at that time, as we were adept at networking more quickly than others, easily located one another, were highly communicative, were efficient, but relegated to carrying the heavy burden and load of most of societal strain, grunt and sophisticated records work and standards, as well as lower wage and high responsibility in managing companies which were at the time, largely not accounting well for their practices, and largely under-regulated, (from w-2s practices to 1099's, and other practices), in small, medium and Corporate-sized businesses. As it was, then, having worked in two counties and coming back full circle to do part-time additional work in investigations in both counties, in the work-school schedule of life, having been repeatedly told how very valuable I was compared to those in society who required heavier screening, the realities were looming and quite telling, with groups of women culminating in local independence and voter leagues, and local campaign-related groups which were concerned about the growing inequalities and looming red herring economic gap, statistically accounted for by local government representatives who were very concerned. One was outraged and ended up leaving the area for Sacramento. One government representative had been holding home town meetings and was present at Corporation group meetings, which regularly met at that time. A lobbyist with them did ask me to run for office for the rights of women, yet I had to pursue my education at that time of crisis. The care of the privileged toward their special interest, and the middleclass being squeezed for its service work with no reward or proper incentivizing provided in careers and jobs was a problem during that time which altogether lasted for 15 years, during my career and education evolution I acquired in three separate counties in the Bay Area, and online. All of this and companies were side-stepping the reality of undervaluing a class of citizens whose contributions were being undervalued on the basis of what can be best classified as an elitist society mentality. It used to be that being an American meant that you had the right to speak freely and to share with others your views about what makes this land great, but those of us who served most profoundly on the front lines of the economy during those years were taught to adopt a an attitude of acceptance mentality, toward those in the general society who were seeking power in business who turned their gaze from economic analysis, to fixate their vision on getting rich, and as fast as they could. These were the days of Gingrich. It was as if the "Gold Rush" was on, and no one could change the thinking of those who were programmed for one thing... pursuit of self-interest. The demands of the self driven often forgot to regard those who were the "machines" who served, some of whose company "ships" of management, or to remain attentive to proper detail, so through the winds of change, would later start moving toward "running aground", shall one say, economically, to leave one inevitably upon new "shores" of business and educational exploration in a Technological Economic revolution. While it has been taught that Marxism taught already the truth concerning social oppression which should not govern societies forever, discovering the Historical truths and the truths of evolving modernity loomed large on the horizon, and were there each waking dawn in the tireless and tiring work of those who put on their boots and marched fearlessly on for as long as they could before utter collapse in later phases and blockades, so to speak, metaphorically, through the haze of American indifference and sometimes, doubletalk. It felt more like Atlas smirked, so to speak, instead of shrugged, in the manufacturing and financial sectors.—(a reference to Ayn Rand's book *Atlas Shrugged*). A Nation cannot go on in blind deregulation before some point of collapse and damage to a number of people, and the covering of it is painful to say the least for those who labor hardest in the fields of life, ultimately, in *good faith* and their *integrity*, as it leaves *good people* with that *unfair burden*. As well, rewarding those who did *not* get the job or career, in some cases, solely based upon merit, is equally an inequality insult in the face of progress, to those who worked harder, when the quality of products goes decidedly down, too, due to changes in management and in the face of indifference, where a whole Nation suffers for it, later, (which includes the *outsourcing* done in America), while poorer nations that America worked harder to bring to its borders, partook of the shrinking economic and medical resources on the shores of an overworked America, whose Baby- Boomers were growing older, with the quality of education equally dropping, in further shift, which severely limited the education and career potentials, of its perhaps *hardest working citizens*. The American Nightmare!, which ought to have been the American Dream, for *them*-America is defined by liberties created in the Constitutional History of a laboring, then, freed Nation, whose meaning became a Nation which under God and Liberty, allowed the *freedoms* and *the blessings of Liberty* to citizens who labored in *good faith* and *fairness* in *fellowship* and *honor, one toward another,* or: The Gift of brotherhood and Prosperity, to "*crown the Good with Brotherhood*", as an American anthem song says, but even this notion was tainted in political rhetoric and attitudes in favor of more and more unregulated business, with the attitude of no gratitude for the "unlucky", which led to the greed, of some, while *decentralized* governance made no allowance for proper 'checks and balances' as it is termed, to keep track of and maintain more properly regulated local business and governance, thus turning a blind eye to valuable business and social statistics, business growth, GDP: Gross Domestic Product; and GNP: Gross National Product, (implying imports and exports and foreign trade), while discrepancies in the maintenance of business practice, which became more and more numerous over time, came about, like a ship not fully maintained or regulated in its running, thus, slowly moving toward running aground, in a manner of speaking. Even the Environmental EPA issues were becoming of interest, in the cities and counties normal infrastructure maintenance, including pollution of air, water and sewage treatment, to much concern of those of us who studied engineering , out of personal interest, along with our interests in business, volunteering with environmental organizations, (over the years); civil engineering and civics, electrical engineering, then later Global Warming, and then participation in leagues concerning local governance issues, city council and local government, and the hiring of truly qualified personnel there and in business, to correct these deteriorative issues, which in some cases required a special, not socially recognized effort. The blindness that seems to accompany those who don't want to see the wisdom in *fairness*, in hiring in the business world, comes full circle to the light of exposure when those persons are caught in ponzi schemes by Congress and Senate, and big government treasury and poorly regulated reserves finally not able to pay the debts created by miscalculating banks, to cover for the faulty loans doled out to persons who were defrauded in false derivative and false double and triple A scandals, let alone a bank scandal of some 4 billion dollars in money laundering in the drug cartels of Mexico, reported in the general media, not to mention fraud in Medicare, which the FBI had to put a literal stop to, along with drug cartels and murder groups, to end severe border battles and smuggling into America, all due to deregulation and the belief that regulating didn't really need to be worried about, but Reaganomics approaches and more deregulation were emphasized, which with healthy regulation could have avoided, as also was the case in the Reagan Economy, if you read and view history and documentaries of statistical reporting in the Media, which problems of that time, as well, could have been more readily avoided, as well as special interest which the Media tells us and statistically, as well as in Hearings, altered business practices, robbed millions if not billions of people of their contributed integrity, their hard earned 401Ks and their dignity, their jobs, their homes and their humanity!- then, on top of it all: Medicare fraud. Some of us endured the double recession crisis that only some people knew about, which actually started in the 1990's, which continued, and many who were in the midst of their same hiring and management practices, both in H.R. and general business, continued in them, well in the years 2000-2006 and beyond, as researched and discussed with H.R. professionals and consultants, confidentially. Studies became more philosophical, as one questions what the definition of Fascism is, and is actually defined as, with more education in Finance, then Philosophy and Sociology, Political Science and History, followed, between my fulltime work load, classes and the continued analysis of Capitalism and Fascism in the large economics picture, and in what circumstances in life, they overlap, in analysis of Economic and Political theory and the direct disciplined reflection upon those disciplines, in life. Each must ultimately decide for one's self, given individual knowledge and experience, regarding good faith what values what one will embrace, in life, during which time, Finance, the Economy and Political theory, then later, Sociology, became subjects of studious interest during that time, in the classroom, with practical experience, in discussion along the way, with colleagues present in the classroom and business, which we "fondly" referred to as "the trenches". Likewise, later in the study of Law and the Constitution, one begins to question how anyone can lay claim to American freedom or being called an "American" when practicing in the name of the Constitution, less than *good faith practice* in business, in America. Even Alan Greenspan warned America all along about the consequences of unchecked regulation before an economics panel of business persons and spoke openly to congress and senate in a governmental review, a number of times, at that time in history, over two years ago, in which Alan Greenspan, quoted from his statistics, forecasting disaster, should America continue on its deregulation course warning about *disproportionate economic consequences* which could affect business, interest rates, and which set about inflation, as I recall in the reported meetings in broadcasts on C-Span. Those on the non-moderated panel laughed, saying that the notion of business being in any way less than "too big to fail", was to them, at that time, preposterous, in a first broadcast, (if you watched any of the broadcasts at all), telling Greenspan it would be best for him to not be so extreme in his thinking, if he could not support heavy deregulation or "progress" because of his fears, in that he was seen as a mild-mannered conservative-minded wall flower, interest rate gate-keeper Economist who was construed to be desirous of holding business back, according to the notions of Reaganomics style of freedom in business practice, and the freedoms of deregulation, as he cautioned businessmen severely, as a professor type that he is, concerning their ideas for massive deregulation and supposed massive "progress" they envisioned, as they allowed deregulation its full course, contrary to his advice, which when the full intoxication of business practice was recovered from, the business "hangover" referred to as such by Senator leaders, I watched recently, in the media in numerous broadcasts, on various channels, on the Senate floor, and whose professional investigative authority in Hearings, was too late to remedy the Greenspan warnings, made to business persons in vain, at last, and even Senate, (observed in a four months segment of time), mostly as noted Republicans themselves, on the Senate floor, who were observed on C-Span, from my eye and ear witness, as I did count the number and did watch to see the party speaking,(used the term "hangover" in fact in their discussions to describe the willful ignoring of advice and pursuit of more deregulated business practice and tax and spend choices), and on C-Span, such persons did say with remorse, on the Senate floor, in flow chart and business discussions of the deficit and business practice and choices made recently in the economy, as well as the long term, that they were sorry they had thought that America was *"too big to fail", right there in Senate! My mouth flung open in shock, I recall, as I was stunned.* Then at the end of two months, later, the same persons and their colleagues were denying and dissociating from the same decisions they had publically expressed remorse for, once again viewed, on the same Senate floor, on a non-moderated C-Span recorded session of Senate, as they stated openly before the Senate floor, to Americans, in more political broadcasts, that they had really not done anything so bad, while they decided to approach a new agenda and to revise their decision, after reviewing the data of facts, right then, to suit their new partisan agenda plan for the Republican promotion of a new approach agenda platform, as I again watched, mouth open, as humble Republican and Democrat

Congressmen, tried to reason how to solve the escalating financial deficit crisis which they finally started to argue about regarding the responsibility issues, and actually were taking more time to analyze where the spending went and what the Bush Administration had actually done, which were discussed in those broadcasts, on C-Span, complete with charts and expressed concerns at the depth of the spending done by the Bush Administration, expressed just in that fashion at that time. Republicans and Democrats, viewed in the Congressional and Senate chambers objectively recorded for broadcast, who are for good faith business practice and follow proper governance, and constitutional rules who have demonstrated concern for our country in their struggle in problem-solving, voiced concerns in meetings, which followed next, fierce discussions and arguments concerning fears associated with management of business and finance, then Hearings gradually thereafter, took place, after the $787 Billion Dollar Bail Out, in that order, to investigate the activities of the financial and regulatory sectors, in the authority's growing discomfort of what they might find, as articulated and investigated at great length in those Hearings. The Gingrich agenda, which lobbied for more deregulation was designed to pave the way for large business, even small business and corporate business interests, in the News at that time, as the goal in sight was to get rich and quick, and to create "progress" and "profits" during a new growth cycle in America, with enthusiasm. Gradually, radio broadcasts suggested that business deregulation seemed to be becoming disproportionate in its broad ranging effects, and that *outsourcing* could present a formidable problem to the economy, but such advice was ignored by moguls and those who *wanted to be* moguls, to join the "progress" agenda Party of businessmen, who had access to special interest constituencies and money. The radio reports mentioned the fear of the notion of big business creating a "permanent underclass", while it found creative ways to "cut corners" on the legislative practices of regulation, during that time, of "progress" during the Bush two terms, as some of us watched numerous broadcasts, nightly and on weekends, the business practices, and incidentally, concerning the practices and attitudes at that time expressed by businessmen as unconcerned about fair (or adjustments needing to be made to) wages, for millions of struggling Americans, most of the top business executives, I noted speaking were Republican. The stats on the particular demographics group of those who suffered economically the most, in the local stats during that time, I also noticed, was being defended by a key number of Democrats at that time as statistics were being revealed and argued about, as well the repetition of this occurrence, in broadcasts, before the final hours of the election statistics and polls outcomes, during the time after the re-election of Bush Jr. . Democrats were pundit targets for the political and economic new Republican agenda of some Republicans who held American legislation in, sort of a freeze, if you will, claiming that they held the golden goose or golden key, and they used those terms interchangeably, in reference to a golden future, at that time, claiming they were the "leaders" who were shaping the nation through business, when in effect their elitist methods and inattention to economics, imports and exports, as well as ignoring Congressional and Senate floor concerns about trade in imports and exports became a heated, intense topic of debate, lobbied about, and details, in oil spills, bad corporate business practices were both fiercely discussed, debated, and often side-stepped, as special interest groups and big business were not concerned about recompensing damages to small business, while merit-based business continued its shift to the right, but rather seeking to get rich in big business and oil business became the overwhelming priority, at the expense of good Americans, in seaside business, health and insurance. The business practices and attitudes in Washington D.C. trickled down to local education as the good, disadvantaged citizens were also targeted further for the agenda of teachers who wanted to add more requirements and keep students in their local education, rather than offering equal access as they themselves had had, as mentioned by a Board of a local State University, who also used the voices of students to lobby for the right of common students to have affordable education, in 2006-2007, as the hard working were having a hard time up the ladder, while encouragement, education and jobs were extended to immigrants, and not necessarily the wealthy, (if you watched it at that time in terms of the priority on Senate floor discussions, and the private agenda motivation among individual businessmen, arguments between the right and the left, and *special interest* now considered unconstitutional. The constituencies among the wealthy, which began to emerge in what is now referred to as "unidentified groups" are being researched presently, for special interest money trails which are considered unconstitutional, which mostly have been in the recent past totally criticized for starting in the Bush Administration, which were then ignored later in the face of deregulation, in the "business as usual" attitude of business and partisanship, which was immediately characterized as "business as usual" and "special interest" by the Senate and the press, if you were watching, then later was fought about in a pundit battle in the next election from Bush to the new administration. Among groups of citizens who were trained on the notion of merit-based opportunity hiring, less than a decade before this shift, a misalignment with front- of- the- line promotion and fair merit-based opportunity occurred, for some in business, which has remained the practice, along with diversity hiring and later *outsourcing* and *loss of jobs* in critical economic growth sectors and districts, until challenged lately, *18 months later,* in the new administration, while other related challenges noted specifically in Arizona that required re-legislation, starting September 24th, 2010 involved re-legislation which Congress decided was much overdue, regarding immigration. This was recorded for C-Span and reported on C-Span. Terrorists threats to America, remain just as detrimental to our Nation, all due to the need for stepped up security and business related policies, to step up regulation, which all has been, after a period of mass deregulation of business and growth cycles, from about 1994 to 2000 and then up to 2008, up to 2009, while Senate and Congress were still reviewing the deficit and business in general, long after government officials took a pay hike in the late 1980's, Americans were told about, after Americans were told they had not been consulted, which again was somewhere about the late 1980's. Service to America was seen by the privileged classes, seemingly, in government as a great gift to humanity, for their good service to America, and their knowledge of the Constitution, as I recall at banquet dinners the speeches which highlighted this discoursed notion, which seemed to tip the scales of reasoning and caused wealth-seeking Americans to follow suit and to see themselves as the bastion of economic pride and profit, as key holders to the American future without limits to growth and wealth potentials, echoing the Reagan era philosophy. American business, while the Nation's budget was already being balanced on the backs of the middleclass, as president G.W. Bush later did business legislation to secure the tax exempt status of the rich in many business contracts and in Corporate America, to secure the tax relief and benefits of capital gains, to wealthy American, along with less overall accountability in big, manufacturing, eventually-(some smaller manufacturing), and Corporate business, was named as "progress", "productivity" and "growth", and, later, special interest became a topic of concern, when many special interest gestures, and special exempt status, seemed to go hand-in-hand, in the Nation's Capital capitalist city compared to most of America, which I saw in business broadcasts, and the very real transformation of some imbalances in management which I saw taking place, in my work and noted among associations of people who differed from myself in their dealings with people, in all of my business experience. As long as one can marry a rich woman, or man, and work and become rich, I noticed that some special interest mentalities could also laugh at middleclass America cynically, without cause to actually hate good Americans, who bid them no rancor. I began to think if sin can be defined as Hypocrisy, and it is, according to the Bible, which was the first foundation for law in villages in the 1200's, according to *my* case law studies, then one should recall Jesus' apt statement concerning hypocrites who later Romans destroyed, due to greed prevalent in the nation, after the fall of Jerusalem, which is part of History, and talked about (in one of my case law classes I took): (of which Jesus said this in scripture): "You go and learn this: (He implied what was at that time desired and needed in behavior in business and worship practice, apparently), which was and is as He defined as a *necessary character trait*: *"you go and learn this: I desire compassion, and not a sacrifice"*. Similarly, "good faith" built the American Nation and its freedoms, with *defense* and *compassion*, in the constitutional *"common defense"* and *"general welfare"*, and laws, which over time, *good faith* was damaged, in a time of compromised faith and eventually ponzi schemes, due to compromised faith in business, poor regulation and unregulated business—which if some people think that good faith has nothing to do with business, or a President who cares about such things, then America has more serious problems than just derivatives and bad insurance policies which were created under an administration which lobbied for endless deregulation, let us not forget! America has always been a land of opportunity. Bankruptcy can kill a Nation and the governing behind what has been recognized in the media as an age in which *unprecedented bankruptcy* has called for *greater legislation* more in this decade than others, due to the need for regulation as the media has pointed out in numerous broadcasts, through Senators in non-moderated broadcasts, of Congressional meetings and Senate floor discussions, non-moderated by the C-Span media with the exception of pauses to examine News breaks and New news updates during Senate floor meetings, for those with an eye that can see that dictatorship or totalitarianism potentials, or greed or the love of money, can, at times, all be the same, depending upon circumstances, economic shifts and opportunity curve shifts which keep small business from their share of American prosperity growth due to preference for other big business growth sector growth, and what that means, religious or not—the meaning is understood in other words, (if you have done your Law; Theology; Political Science and Business studies, as well as the Math Statistics and watch the Economy and Hearings in the News Media, and in business, and Wall Street figures, as well, the objective courtroom Hearings, about what happened in the Financial sectors, as well), then you too, know what I am making reference to. When I used to hear the "read my lips" speech about no new taxes, I knew that the purport of the message was meant to take power and to deregulate to an extent businessmen felt necessary and proper, but I felt within myself, that such deregulation, at that time, might become dangerous due to inattentiveness inherent in humanity and the love for profits, already present in business, and I could tell by the laughter and jokes toward people what that could mean to the economy, as it frightened me then, *before* the former President was elected. I rightly feared what eventually did happen in the Economy. People make decisions, and inherently, people can make rash decisions with blinders on, regarding the disregard of the equal need of proper regulation. People rationalize toward and in favor of their desired outcomes, often rather than practicality for the total economic balance, because people love to make money, without restraint. Where disabled persons have not even enough food to allow them to stand up, for example, low blood sugar disables them from thinking straight, but that is not the same thing at all, if you have studied people, clinically. Not enough food leads to two types of disorders, but *inattentive* people can fail to see the need for *consumer protection* and *regulation*, which is literally what happened, as mentioned by the Senate and Congress in another broadcast on C-Span after some of and still during the $787 Billion Dollar Bail Out Hearings conducted by Barney Frank, Judd Gregg, Senator Kyle, Senator Waxman, Senator Menendez, and others. Essentially, persons can tend to side on the side of their *wishes* often, in human nature, instead of finding always the most democratic and balanced regulated ways and means of doing business, but rather, quickly and easily, when as such, business is performed and not regulated, or loosely regulated, where money interests are concerned. The meaning of Democracy is *equal participation and voting* in any society, philosophically speaking, since the days of the Greeks, in History.

At last, just the other evening, September, the 24th, to be exact, in this year of 2010, re-regulation concerning immigration laws practice only recently began to take place, as it were, reported in the News Media Sept. 24th on C-Span, where the Senators all came together and made a concerted effort to praise the immigrants who have served well and fed America well, as well as those who have become educated and are productive citizens. Next, the very real issues of legislative importance were raised regarding the laws needing to be written in such a fashion as to address the very real overdue concerns of crime, drugs and other problems coming across borders which threaten our American way of life, safety, and take jobs from citizens who are already living in America, who have been here a long time and deserve the jobs for being residents here already, as stated by the Senators –that is, those citizens who have priority, at *the front of the line*, as stated by the Senators. *Outsourcing* as we know *caused many jobs to be sent overseas*. There seem to have emerged two types of persons in America: Those who are interested in good faith, good business, opportunities and prosperity for Americans, and those who seem to have self and personal as well as special interest in mind, in seeking to procure what they want for themselves, regardless of the impact on the lives of others, which we have seen in health, wages and outsourcing, oil spills, corporate hearings of numerous kinds, which is what America seems to be becoming, since the surplus of Clinton and the Bush eras of catering to those who are at the advantage, who have had consistent access, and have allowed preference for *privilege* to shape part of our modern economic recent history, favoring those at the advantage and skipping certain Americans who are next in line, for merit career positions, I have noticed, and as regards proper tax laws, the desire to let only some pay, while poverty line statistics reported static wages in general social statistics throughout two recessions. These are Social Statistics researched and completed for course work and reported to local governance in hometown meetings and city, and county professionals. This social-economic favoritism  to preserve access for the wealthy, usually includes the top 10% of society and those who own 90% of the wealth, which trend started back in the 1980's as stated in general social and derivative statistics, when schools often fell too far short of meeting the demands of business and students, to satisfy the demands of the working world, (which did not include those of us who mastered our career skills (although the trend was by no means true in all schools)- especially private schools, when there were economic crises associated with the outsourcing which created the economic instability, at least, in California, which I and associates have personally seen, along with the student loan scandals, in record numbers which have swept the Nation, of concern to Congress and Senate, as mentioned in a number of broadcasts in Congress and Senate. (I had been asked to run for an office locally within groups of corporate women and with local voting league voters, who expressed concerns about the quality of life for women and the state of affairs in the economy and education, also the same concerns as in hometown meetings with governmental legislators, who also relocated to Sacramento and Washington D.C., not more than five years ago, from my district, or, in 2005). The battles created due to these oversights and non-Constitutional non-considerations has been intolerable for many as it is, and is referred to in Sociology statistics, and open broadcast radio and media statistics which are largely the same, I find, in their findings, recently reported and in the four years mentioned. Many schools in California make it impossible for some people to gain a fair and equitable education as there is mass discrimination upon persons who are disadvantaged, poor and could never afford loans, but need an education. I just raised these issues with school officials recently where some programs favor the wealthy who are in a high affordability bracket and can actually manage loans, while certain persons definitely cannot and are in hardship brackets, beyond what "normal" students can imagine. Obviously, business and education are important topics and should have been addressed a very long time ago in fact, by business, Congress and Senate, through enforced legislation, as we have witnessed a decline of values in the American culture and Economy—not just the Baby Boomer generation issues are of concern, here, but as well, the fabric of life as we know it and educational stability for all citizens, which has declined steadily or eroded for the past 8 years, specifically, I have noted, and six years specifically in the Bay Area, before that, as I have steadily researched colleges, universities and state universities in all fifty states, for the last five years, all told, 14 years in public school, not private school, and access to it, (for some citizens), and many statistics concerning costs and Pell coverage, out- of- control costs, which distress Senators, I also have watched in these last four months of August, September, October and November, 2010, which were mentioned in brief, in March, 2010, in the new administration of the year transitioning after the election from 2009 to 2010. Legislation began to address the ignored issues of fiscal regulation which had been discovered by the Senate to have been ignored for too long. Allowing parts of a population to become essentially less educated, or worse, endangered, according to statistics, is no boon to a bust economy as even Mr. Alan Greenspan made very clear to warn us against creating such a scenario, in the media, as mentioned earlier in this book, and present economists warn us about this continually as a Nation, and did warn us, before the economic crash of the years 2000-2008, while under the leadership of George Walker Bush. Status quo has much to do with the values the society espouses: Education and I.Q. is *far more important as a philosophy*, as well as *sane and sound* affordability, than numbers or *heads to be taxed* without regard to protections to humanity, their health, what they can afford, differences in population demographics and economic brackets and providing greater fair and balanced work and education opportunities in an imperfect, evolving world, for *above average and literate Americans*, which will only cause more problems in the society, if not addressed, and is *central* to moving toward *success* in *any* country and economy— and America is learning this the hard way. If you fail to recall History and the 1950's, education and what happened back then, then you are doomed to repeat it— Not honoring the needs of people hurts the Nation and its Gross Domestic Product and its Gross National Product. Look at Finland on National broadcasts: They love their people and teach them *well*, *honoring* teachers and pay attention to keeping costs *affordable*, which is why they are *leaders* in the *World Economy* concerning *Education* and *Economic Productivity*. Economic parity has become greed in America. If not administering education for the sake of education, and honoring all people and women, as well, the grave fact of those who are indeed *more disadvantaged*, will mean entrenched poverty and no way out, as such persons *indeed*, *cannot afford* loans in education, as others may be able to, as a statement of how people differ in the world and not all persons are vocational persons, by any means, or will be able to fit into that role or the limited vocational jobs sector in manufacturing, if more jobs come back, nor are some the computer systems types or I.T. types of persons for those industries. They are just *not* that *type* of people or mental *talent!* You simply cannot force a round peg into a square hole, so to speak, regarding some persons, (certainly not all persons, as some are well-suited and need mere encouragement), and where community colleges fail to serve certain types of students whose learning style is eclectic and essentially not technically routed in its overall *orientation* to *communications, speed and agility regarding specifically bundled course work*, and technical learning. I should think that College Institutions would understand this basic premise concerning *personality types* and disadvantage concerning socially different styles of learning and social interaction styles, as well as and overall college prep, which has been different for older and disenfranchised persons who cannot go back to schools they are too mature and educated to attend, where cultures are too different and technical courses now out of date, too fast and out of step with the now developed style of the one track minded software mastery approach in learning schools have fostered, while those who worked and went to school, survived in companies, burned out from years of service and inadequately compensated to afford anything but assistance for college, as they could not afford food without assistance in education. No desperate person will take out a loan when they are starving. Education priorities were *indeed* priorities back in the 1950's, as well as a merit-based, productive and an attentive society, which built secure infrastructure with *good faith* practice. I am a Social Scientist mentality and student concerning statistics, as well as a student of Psychology statistics, and in clinical as well as societal analysis, with a career background in business and management, including accounting and H.R. management and business leadership, formerly. The privileged were given every opportunity that some of us, have had to painstakingly eke out and my status of person in education and career strata faced and will face the continued uncertainty of work which Senators target as a looming crisis in the future, just around the corner, according to the inside Congressional and Hearing debates among Senators and Congressmen—I am not without the support of those in deep agreement on this point, among educators, even in California schools, at present, and I had written and lobbied former Governor Schwarzenegger about keeping a good school open, which he did. If you watch business since the 1980's and 1990's, business got more constrained and limited in opportunities in about 1994, with transitions toward the Hi-Tech "superhighway" which was paved with the lives of those of us who worked in management for those who managed and outsourced America beyond the scope of routine business practice, across the province of predictable economic profits and needed regulation, and routine management's *choice to send jobs elsewhere* when, in fact, business was not *"too big to fail"* as they had claimed representatives felt it was not, as certain representatives had claimed, as businessmen, they had squandered opportunities within and for America. While city infrastructures try to compensate for management practices by hiring more apt personnel in Human Service, and Criminal Justice, while creating more costs to maintain new security for more crime levels, business if managed differently may have produced very different results in the economy and social structuring, as well as the products and the services in the infrastructures of cities. Human Resources were likewise hired, per city, cutting Social services, which they drastically did, the homeless increased, in the changing economic repercussions and the downturn cycles. This cycle by far, is the *worst* I have have ever witnessed through the years. What helps to build a city infrastructure is to consider the security and safety needs first, with revenues, business development, and business infrastructure, accountability, then housing, usually in that order, as, if you have difficulty with revenue streams, you will have difficulty building real estate value, commercial real estate and business, Education will thus suffer and people's ability to pay for it, in a devalued structure and society of people, and jobs, with the smaller manufacturing businesses suffering the loss of revenues, with the increased need for more taxes to compensate, to rebuild infrastructure. Only large and corporate business can really pick up that slack in the larger equation, in the face of such a *huge economic crisis*, even if the crisis was softened in its blow, by the economics intervention to stop a full blown second Great Depression! So, relieving the wealthiest of taxes is *hugely unrealistic*, in that, at this time of the Economy, even with smaller taxes and better planned tax structures, even with any wealth dividend losses, with the middleclass issues, and population problems, be it unemployment and infrastructure building being huge issues of their own, large business and Corporate taxes are still necessary *as a large majority of people just don't have the money that the top* 10% *and top* 20-40% *have*, in having the advantage, if you study the economics basics in society. Plus, the wealthy have enjoyed the tax breaks and advantages in the last two terms of the previous administration under Bush and have a comfortable lifestyle. It is time for a change, *purely economically speaking, let alone, socially speaking.* Most people are easy targets however, because they have not heard nor had time to watch and review or listen to radio, or T.V. in many case instances, to informative and savvy broadcasts, on a regular basis, which are objective and non-moderated, but strictly reporting the facts, such as on regular recent C-Span broadcasts and 88.5 recent and former broadcasts. Pundits and partisan thinkers just seem to love that, as it tends to feather the special interest nest for those at the advantage. One has to wonder just *how many people really understand this principle of socio-economics- that is, partisan nest-feathering, in light of best balanced business and fair tax strategy, and why the rich can afford those taxes. Better put, how fair is it to allow some people, only, to have access to a future, while others are told they must eternally carry the burden and for all the limiting profit choices made by some small, and large manufacturers, as well as Corporate businesses and choices, which the overburdened clearly cannot afford. Big business and Corporations have forever changed business and profit potentials, in the now recognized style of business and business models and outsourcing, in now global competition, which thus limits profit potentials for some business and jobs sectors! While I do consider myself a social science, and economics mentality, one needs to understand that big business created the need for government regulation in business, finance and medicine, by keeping the low wage earner in the low percentage poverty statistics demographics, by not rewarding merit for service, with further merit and proper education as well as opportunities that it lavished upon the preceding generation of semi-educated and educated as well as more advantaged privileged classes, while skipping some semi-educated professionals, while skipping some semi-educated professionals they further made disadvantaged Americans, in the process, and allowing business to charge as much as they could get away with, with little to no regulation upon their practices, which got out of control. The disenfranchisement of the "unlucky", the privileged created, in essence, therefore, by creating and deepening the poverty statistics in this Nation, in their business practices and outsourcing, while prices and rates of imports, exports and currency exchange, escalated and were not properly managed, nor regulated, (in that order), to the best advantage of American business, consequently, those who labored at home on the shores of America were marginalized in many cases. The devalue of* *service in products and service in manufacturing and service for those who were aspiring toward a future, in business and through education, particularly in insurance and heath, as well as other industries, for whom services were originally created as well, were depriving some citizens of proper service, some of which Americans were paying for, due to no regulation of such, and the service fees went above livable rates, unchecked, for far too many Americans, which cannot be justified. Many healthcare companies did this too, unknown by the American general population of the status quo. Standards price rates were raised and value standards fell, in business practice, and I don't mean in reference to <u>Standard and Poor's</u>.* In today's world, there is no incentive for people to do unusually good things for any society in America, anymore, it seems, among disadvantaged Americans in particular—people, who want to do good in society these days, tend to be cynically underappreciated and shunted aside! *When will America learn this?* This creates unrest and also contributes to crime in management and poor values in service business sectors, and in other places in society, in so many other ways- as we have recently seen with the Banks, SEC securities, the Federal Reserve, and then the financial sectors in their ponzi schemes, finally!, as reported in C-Span broadcasts.

The real challenge of *this* age, is to reconcile the incessant errors, and to face the challenge to integrate knowledge, in the use of technical interface, as well, in Technical computer communication platforms where people need to communicate more and more effectively—enough to have full understanding of what they are in complexity troubleshooting in the software and use of codes or keys that deal with security issues which all came about due to the industrial information age transition, with a shift toward less preoccupation with product or service excellence, as opposed to preoccupation with code and database management protocols, over time, when using data information streams in data industries, which evolved for a period of time. This disconnect has cost America in profits, in security and more hacking/cracking and investigation, webpage fraud and other schemes, long after the early days of FORTRAN and DOS systems when information used to be painstakingly eked out by persons, once again, who had a *concern* for well running systems, due to a collective mental evolution of some persons in the working world who have tried to evolve knowledge, information systems and a steady flow of well-integrated knowledge streams. Some of us have helped to manage them into existence with service. This is crucial in that for a "well-oiled" economy to run well, the "gears" of information and communication have to be synchronized to work lockstep, integrated, in conjunction with consistent facts and ways/means of using and running programs, and data systems and databases, which due to schemes and management styles, underwent some changes in systems and processing of data. Databases changed right about the years 1990-2000-2001-2 from what I could see of them, and Networks, and essentially the I.T. industry split off as another industry alternative for employment in the general economy, much as the Green Technologies and Telecommunications as well as GIS has become now. I.T. became used as a tool for some to store vast data as well as others to refine data for larger better purposes. Essentially, change of data structures, purpose and storage size which changed before and with the I.T. industry, continued.

Understanding how to integrate the scientific and sometimes spiritual dimensions with the material and informational is challenging, but is integrated insofar as a person may encounter integrated end users and apt teachers of these protocols of software in systems use, and their individual philosophies of business practice and life. So, language and communication became divided I suppose one could say, somewhere around 1995 or so, before the Search Providers decided to upgrade their services and to see their providers as valuable and needing a bit of upgrade improvement to save important information as for example in tools files and URL references with email features to save and retrieve information for easy recollection and access. Some of us, who are communicators by nature, wanted those features to be available *before* they were, and certain media providers were becoming more popular than others then others began to appear on the scene as well. Why this is so important is because communication needs to be integrated in order to be valuable rather than disjointed, for it to be practical to use by *everyone*, in a global economy. But then what about elements in the society that challenge our security? What then? So has evolved the General Security forces, P.D. forces, Homeland Security and how to regulate to keep ahead of undesirable elements in any economy which is certain to develop, as business grows.

The information age evolution and systematic deregulation led to much chaos, company inefficiencies, albeit successes, where production and output and database management was less supervised, in some cases, for which I had to supervise and account for general company accountability in certain places, while seeking to improve business practice, for overall productivity, which drew attention to the need for regulation which looked toward fairness for businesses and consumers, which was a challenge, due to needing to keep up with the get rich way of business and life, practiced by many and not directly shared by some, which practices changed the fabric of life insofar as larger businesses started a business pathway trend which fostered growth. However, with outsourcing came the inevitable sending away of jobs, with poorer attention to detail among some systems and databases, groups and structures, and with it, inevitably, the quality in local manufacturing and even other types of businesses in Silicon Valley, which practices in some places, disrupted the way of life for other sectors as described in this text in detail above and previously, on the last eight pages, significantly, in reference to education and economics, and could have been avoided. The trend of general business, seemed to set about careless online web advertising, by some sources, scams of numerous proportions, mixed with legitimate ones, and general non- accountability in business, which fostered crime and the taking advantage of the middleclass and other cultural class sectors, up until about 18 months ago, when the new administration was in full swing and then when jobs were noted to begin to surface first in the private sector, and then later, the public sector. When the jobs were filled, the incumbent administration was unjustly blamed for jobs productivity in America, dropping. The problem had been created by the *outsourcing*. Communication in business, became for the exclusive use and manipulation of persons who in having some difficulty keeping up with demand in business, phones and paperwork and emails, were less and less (in many cases) accountable to get back to other people and tended in some cases to prefer a less communicative approach to business style of accountability, which set about a noticed "epidemic" or overall style of ignoring getting back to persons in the business sector, as noted, up until about four months ago specifically, as watched and noted online, in business and on jobs websites. Doing things based upon merit was eventually replaced, or so it seemed, with a political façade and inattention to emails and communication, on too many occasions to ignore (in just the performance of routine business), until there was a fair amount of gridlock at one point, until 18 months ago, when the gridlock began to loosen up during an extremely tense, crisis economy which was riddled with depression and hostility, locally and at the Capital city of our Nation. Personal gain was the focus, it seemed. While some other types of businesses worked harder and flourished better, it also seemed, two things occurred: The imports/exports sector became unclear about taxation in duties and excises to be levied, and concerning the G20 Summit, with the WTO: World Trade Organization legislation, unsure of how to conduct itself in the global schema of the Political Global Front, understandably. While the technical products in Hi-Tech which were thought to be a leader and would lead to a greater boom, they did not lead to the boom expected, and some of this involved the ignoring of duties in exports and imports, concerning the economy, and analysis of it which took place indeed, during the Bush administration, specifically, noted, *then*. The dot com industry bubble burst suddenly and the rush to get rich quick in this way was suddenly seen for the industry it really was- often unstable and unpredictable, yet beneficial to *some*. Some of the privileged had gotten rich at the expense of the worker and "gotten out of dodge", so to speak, or consolidated in mergers to stay in business, and took their business elsewhere, while finance and real estate followed in doing business in a manner in enough cases, which was damaging, leading to the near collapse of the economic structure, due to deregulation and inattention to proper regulation, which was discovered and mentioned later by economists, senators and governmental Hearing specialists in numerous non-moderated recorded C-Span broadcasts. Prosperity was limited, locally in the job market I found, while researching it, locally, and globally, and local government seemed hard to get answers from, seeming uncaring, like the business world felt in itself "too big to fail". The whole mess might have been avoided with the exception of what seems man's inherent desire for power, and love of money, which seemed to fuel the fires of indifference and rapid negative change in some business practice—(Thankfully not in all). Businesses closed. I had warned a number of Hi-Tech, product and service related businesses that they would be likely to experience difficulties, as they used their style of trying to "consult" in their services as everyone wanted to manage and get rich. In some cases, eventually people took their business elsewhere before properly being consulted, when the cynicism reached its summit and apex, as is always the case in business. Hacking and cracking increased and the same tactics were used online in advertising and emails, as it went unchecked and unregulated until overdone, in cycles, and then technical reforms on main search engines and other windows and webpage based programs, and communications online were made more streamlined, as another industry slowly emerged.

Overall, since 1996, the trend has been to increasingly adopt standards of deregulation which is not limited by any means to business. It also has affected government to the extent that almost all business had come to a standstill eventually, as noted in some areas in the economy or "gridlock" in local effectiveness in business, as business slowed in some cases, in California, before the State deficit hit in 2006-2008 in many sectors, which is why it was so important to usher in a statesman for President, (or a Senator), who would turn around the common multi-legislation challenge, to set about reformation in and around the business market, which to me at that time there seemed very obviously the need for, as I saw in business at that time- (before the presidential election of the Senator). We all know who that Senator is. Individual Senate bills translate into better City/County and infrastructure improvements, even in our local cities which have taken at least four years, per city to do, with great speed in 18 months, in my neck of the California woods- for those of us who know our cities.

As the economy improves, I find that people are in a state of willingness to be a success and to make life a success for others. What we need is to remain positive despite the obvious challenges we face as a Nation. I feel I must encourage like a stateswoman about it, and in our changing world, women have to step up to the challenges as well, and try to improve the business sectors as they can, but nicely, as the city you save, will be your own. Of that I can speak, personally and publically, after being asked to run for local office through a league, concerning women's issues, just in our city, while I meet local business owners and introduce locals to one another to address mutual business needs in services at present. I recall in desperation, campaigning in our city supervisor myself and making city changes in the local neighborhood, helping business with personal efforts in marketing and advice for business growth and recommending local bank-assisted accounts online advertising, to local business owners, in good faith, while telling restaurants about available property space they were delighted to know they could consider, they had not time to know was even empty and available on the market, as I would drive past them, in my area. This was for the purpose of improving business and also advertising business services better, through the newly regulated banks and perks like free online advertising until maybe fees could be tolerated. (I never had time to find out), and to grow local business while continuing research, was the ongoing effort, which is still ongoing with work and education still, education and grants, again adjusted by the incumbent President Obama, to make e education affordable, which for me, would not be possible if not for the new President. I write and receive letters from the President in his indomitable style which we hear on the weekly updates on television, FDR style, which are reassuring. I had painstakingly voted in other city council members when my friend had retired from the council and I continued to help in Voter Registration, years afterward. My friend in City Council local government had been so perfect in the chamber as well, locally. It was very hard to see her go in our very small, and yes, more quiet city, which is yes, still developing! Yes, seeing to having mentioned the need for the installing of two more grocery stores for the growing population, by asking a known city council member I voted in, along with another colleague of his, on the Council, was for me, was necessary thing, given the population growth which had taken place locally over an 8 year time frame. People can be heard. I am proud to have helped small business evolve, in some way, and to bring business to some local businesses, despite my individual life, in being busy just living and surviving/studying and needing to fulfill my American Dream, myself, in the Bay Area which is hard enough, strangely.

Most recently, I had been doing telecommuting part-time, in addition to everything else, with a Private Investigator's office, which is in Private Industry, (after completing studies with a legitimate and well supported Investigations school, based out of Massachusetts), whose leader is part of a prominent network association of investigators with an impressive background, verified by local authorities as genuine. The father of the investigator worked for Desert Storm troops, back in 2002-2006 or so I think it was, as well. With this unending Iraqi war going on as it has been now, for about 4 years, plus, we have a new president of 18-22 months, by the time this small account "memoire" of mine is read, I have followed all the ponzi and derivative and insurance account schemes and scams fostered by fraud and legitimate business that I have seen reported or heard of in the Congressional Hearings and meetings, as well, online, and on internal Hearings broadcasts- Just the Hearings- non-moderated, that I have witnessed/researched, which Congress and Senate Hearings have taken place now, to correct the unnecessary evils we could have better avoided since before 2006, which I have been following in numerous broadcasts over the space of nearly two years, in the News on C-Span objectively listening to the non-moderated recorded Hearings and other broadcasts, particularly this last 18 months, which have included the updates on Goldman Sachs; Lehman Brothers; AIG obviously, the SEC, Treasury, Fanny Mae and Freddie Mac. I also watched Justice Proceedings and relegislation to correct the problems vies' a vee committee Hearings and *many* of them, as well as other Banks and institutions which are still under some scrutiny, which is still on the Washington D.C. agenda. I had known and sensed the impending disaster before Alan Greenspan had mentioned it, and I had watched him myself and before Congress as Congress had met in the Senate about it as well, on numerous recorded non-moderated occasions. America had had a choice to go a different path if they had decided to. Businessmen's individual interests and deregulation in favor of big business, the wealthiest, were what tipped the scales in Washington D.C., and not Democrat's wishes, over concerns about the economy and economic looming disaster, to be very frank, as I watched at the edge of my chair as all the worst loan scandal News later broke, and was revealed, segment by segment! On the other hand, many persons had also made investments they clearly could not afford, which was part of the get rich schemes and derivatives/ insurance and Real Estate era of fraud, poor credit and fast decisions era, roughly 2002-2008 and then 2009, culminating into the $787 billion dollar bail out. Then the Senate Hearings began, later when the public was also informed of what had gone wrong, which after another State and National election, America had put someone new in charge—that is, a new President, and well, "business as usual" had to begin to *change*, as it started to, with numerous bills of legislation in Washington D.C., statewide and in business, as I did follow the slow progress, and did watch all the main Senators and Representatives in every State, for 18 months, and had during altogether, the previous 4 years, in every C-Span update report available, and there have been many, long before the President Obama was voted into office, and before the Bi-Partisan wars in Washington D.C. and the election. C-Span has recorded the *true* facts in all their non-moderated broadcasts *I watched*, as none of the Hearings were moderated, as well. While one party was blamed almost solely for the plight of America, it *truly* needs to be noted that the plight of America was first started on that path, by those with enough money who had the power to get rich, and the responsibility to account for themselves, who, in fact, did try to make America a one party agenda for business freedom from taxes, as observed on the Senate floor, until the statesman was voted into office, to turn the tide of history, away from a second Great Depression in American History, (if one follows and knows recent History and the legislated bills: Republican, AND Democrat). World War I, World War II, and European History as well as that of the Middle East and Peace processes are also past and present History which I am acquainted with. One must be consumed and absorbed by Political Science to keep abreast of these events, legislation and News, as well as have a deep interest in Law and Justice, overall, and love our military. I have said to many in the city I live in: "The city you save will be your own". (One must keep this in mind, in times of economic difficulty and infrastructure evolutions). I had located the Investigator I had a stong interest to work for locally, and gone in to meet him after a cold call discussion, and after I had finished some studies with an online Investigations School, which is a legitimate school, run by an Investigator who is professional and has been practicing for many years, and started the school. I then studied Insurance at a small inexpensive public, private, amazingly, family-owned and *professional* school, to get updated on Insurance and business details and practice, and the industry, *preliscenced* and up on *code and ethics* before I took a *real look* at the current market and trends, just to see how much market damage indeed had been done. Much damage had been done. So much damage, that fraud was mentioned in the open market which was reported to me in the school as a concern, and in the general market, to me, as a seeker. Market hysteria had set in. People were afraid to buy and to commit to companies. The owner of the investigations school I had taken an interest in studying with had been backed by the Association of Investigators and Officers Association. I located him after numerous phone calls in my area, due to unrest in the market. Essentially, communities have grown in great importance over the years, in our emerging global economy. It is not for nothing that Oversight Reform specialist Senator Darrell Issa, of Security, economics and Treasury work as well as Social Security management, mentioned in a meeting before the media and before a second Heritage Foundation Committee meeting on Social Security and Tax reform, telling the people of his experiences, and in the meeting, recorded by C-span, in a meeting broadcast, (not moderated), broadcasted on September 30th 2010, stating that in his experiences in law, the military and in security, working on budgets and with Social Security, that one "must raise taxes to pay for Social Security", and if the workers of America have their salaries adjusted to pay for it all, e.g. "without taxing the top 200k-250k" earners- (These are his words): that Social Security: "could not exist" upon which some and more groups than you might imagine must depend upon to survive, due to their place in the economic structure, and those who are in the next phase of the economic growth cycle have their feet well on the path into their economic future, and the next generation. So, without that taxation, we would essentially have too big a burden and "not be able to afford it" if the taxes are not imposed, (*in his own words*), *stated above*. He went on to say that big business had to be "taxed" so that the "gap" could "close" and citizens could also save their social security in the future. Those are his words, quoted. So, it is interesting that some persons can take the "deficit" information and derive somehow that *less* taxes should be charged, and essentially, it is really more the case to assert that small business needs a break, and yet, large business owners and Corporations are continually referred to as the entities which need to pay taxes responsibly, due to their *superior earning and profit status*, (by the educated professionals) such as Darrell Issa and economists, particularly Divergence statistics economists. The institutions which are the largest and therefore the most capable entities of supplying the "reasonable tax" , as stated, "rather than an overall universal flat tax", as stated by Darrell Issa, is more "appropriate"—in essence, the overall *reasonable tax* paid by the wealthy who have *enjoyed* the *freedoms* in business to *have* their private surplus and a *higher lifestyle*, as they can *contribute something back* to the Economy, Constitutionally speaking, and concerning the provisions put in place for America, so as to allow America to flourish like a "well-oiled" machine, to sustain growth, have reserves for training and educating, to allow mutual opportunities for the poor who are developing within our Nation, and small businesses, and those who deserve the same opportunities as those who have received their education a long time ago, and have *the blessings of liberty*, Constitutionally speaking, that *others* also *want and need*, which is their Constitutional Right in America, and has always been the case in America, for the purpose of fostering continual prosperity, by law and duty, to help to sustain the economic and Constitutional needs of the United States economy, to sustain the needs of aging Baby Boomers, and those in need of proper education toward *a realistic and sustainable future*, as well as to keep fluid the markets; Real Estate and Foreign Trade structures concerning imports and exports and necessary duties as well, which WTO: The World Trade Organization provisions in conjunction with China were in fact not addressed to closure, and full resolution toward established agreements not achieved under the G.W. Bush administration, as should have been done in the interest of good and strategic, wise attentive business practice, for proper trickle down, and Yen, Yuan management as stated by economists. But rather as the updated report of the Washington D.C. Divergence Economics update indicates, in the Sept 30 report: It details the difference between *"the 3% trickle down to the poor, among the poverty and 'wealth gap' "* which *"emerged during the early 1990's and 1970's"*, and before that time, due to tax breaks put in place which at that time adjusted and offered *Capital Gains benefits in legislation*, for the wealthiest Americans and Corporations, allowing a whopping *"9% trickle down, to Corporations"* and Big Business and more trickle down to the *already secure and consistently profiting business Americans* who are the top 10%, who *own* the *wealth* of the *Nation* in the *wealthiest Nation* in the *world*, as outlined in general business and social statistics, economics, divergence statistics reported by Washington D.C. economists, and proved in numerous public private party gathering Bi-Partisan discussions on the lawns of city backyards, which President Barack Obama has participated in, two of which I watched in the last week of September, which was between Sept. 20th and Sept. 30th 2010, in the update objective reports of what has been done that was objectively accounted for, during the campaign, in which, open forum, question-answer style, in every such type of broadcast I have personally witnessed on television. He makes reference to the same set of facts and policies as well as the same procedures for his method of correcting the economy, consistently, and what he followed through to correct in the economic disasters which were bequeathed him by the former Bush Administration, that *deficits* were so deep as the demographics charts I have seen attest, that he had very few choices and made the best choices that he absolutely could make during the first moments, months and 18 months all-together in office, as difficult as those were, running from one situation to the next, literally, of America's financial crisis, then coming out of crisis in America, in 18 months, on the verge of a Depression! The radio broadcast on 88.5 KNPR radio outlined from Washington D.C. Gwen Ifill, who reports as well on the National News, but in this report was heard along with top economists she was interviewing, to echo their claim in making clear, their assertions, that *"taxation must take place, at the top, among the 200k-250k earners in the Nation, to make up for the huge economic 'gap' between the rich and the poor which currently exists"*. The Economists who spoke are pure statisticians. They have no political agenda. It is about *numbers, strictly*. It is not just the plan of the President Obama to exact this action, which is not Partisan in the decision made, but rather an Economic logistic, to avoid disaster, which is a necessity as outlined by the Economic and Security professionals who have years of professional experience. As Senator Darrel Issa, Specialist in Security and Treasury/Social Security and Oversight Administration, as well as the Airforce, also did mention, it is important to have continued *"regulation"* in place to deter the *"natural tendency"* toward *"laxity"*, which are his words, which those items he mentioned are prevalent and common knowledge that such institutions and business leans toward laxity when it comes to economic security maintenance, as business tends to ebb and flow in its normal processes, which I think is a very interesting commentary on the nature of business and security as well as regulation in this Nation. It is not hard to have government in business present to regulate it, Senator Darrel Issa reminded us, but that rather America *"has gotten slowly away from responsible attentiveness"* to these procedures, as in the Reagan era, he claimed that President Reagan *"paid a price for not being attentive enough to the need for proper regulation"*, as such, the cold war was "a clever way for Reagan", he claimed, to "reclaim" himself after some legislative steps Reagan took at that time, which G.W. Bush did also in his politics, which Bush's legislative policies were leading the country toward the inevitable process of deregulation that President Bush fostered for the ease toward so much fluidity for the wealthy, albeit for some business, and Corporations, that regulation was as Senator Issa puts it: *"for too long, ignored"* to the point of "detriment". So, what we now are told is that *the ignoring of the regulation should have been attended to, but* was rather ignored so that business could be free to make as much money as they wished, (making money, essentially, not being a bad thing), but also, to not be accountable, contrariwise, is terrible and detrimental and leads to less attentiveness in more focused foreign trade, calling for the wiser decision: taxation and business development strategies which can better foster growth in business, globally, so there should be less deficit spending which the Bush Administration did a lot of spending, as Senator Issa points out in that broadcast, in ways which regulation and taxation would have made business more effective and discouraged many of the escalating problems had there been more attentiveness which, continued deregulation finally led to the thinking that business was "too big to fail", but business did in fact fail, and as observed in the statistics, led to the allowance of those with constituent influence, or "constituency interests" that Issa made reference to, a key factor in therefore setting the Nation up for eventual "crisis", and economic fall, along with inattentiveness to deregulation, interest rates, export and import duties, which the word "crisis" was the word Darrell Issa used, himself, which he claimed "could have been avoided" and "now needs to be avoided" in the future, in his professional opinion, in the meeting with the Heritage Foundation, which is an economic institution of research, of collegiate as well as governmental institutional excellence, in the September 30, 2010 C-Span broadcast. (Not C-Span 1).

The way that business was executed in fact, politically, allowing deregulated business to remain as such, to the extent that inattentiveness to basic laws and regulation for safety and proper Constitutionality and legislative policy, changed this Nation from a free society of progress and possibility, to scams, less freedom and prosperity, to fear and unrest, the need for more security and investigation, which generated more costs for citizens and government, due to greed for profits by some, and negligence in attentiveness to excellence by others, (not by all in business), which led to the degradation of good general business practice in some cases, to outright corruption, overall, loss, and homelessness as well. For when not in good faith united, we as a Nation, become divided and fall. United we stand in principle of ethics and good business practice, but when not in that Unity toward Prosperity, *we* as a Nation and People do fail. As stated by legal investigative professionals and Senators, as such, Banks sought out cheap and rather quick ways to do business to satisfy their ends and means, so as to cut corners in regulation, as mentioned to me by a Banker classmate in Insurance class, and mismanagement in banking fees began to take place in certain fees situations, then industry fraud in derivatives loans, which was reported on C-Span in their Washington D.C. objective *Journal* broadcast of Sept. 30th, 2010 at 4:47 Pacific Standard time and 7:48 Washington D.C. time, (as recorded, on the broadcast). Robert Gates then feared a wider gap between the Nation, and the Military, while the war was seen as an "abstraction", in this grizzly war of Iraq. Where was it leading? Many of us suspected it was leading to some kind of lasting progress such as had taken place in the civil wars of America's 1800's, concerning the Confederacy. No one was certain.

Republican Ken Brady on *Washington Journal* of the Ways and Means Joint Economic Committees, on the GOP proposals On Taxes and Spending, said that *Republicans "spent too much money and that lessening taxes is the best way to curb deregulation."* However, he failed to make clear the reality that the rich in this recession can afford to be reasonably taxed at their yearly average earnings level of "200k-250k", and that he claims *unjustly* that Democrats will use that as an excuse to tax the middleclass, when in effect all other broadcasts and Congress as well as Senate internal floor and office discussions showed just the opposite in the intent of the Democrats, if you watched, and rather that the Republicans in the legislative bills were holding the middleclass "hostage", and the Democrats had not made any such attempt to do any such thing in legislation, but rather, the opposite, as they had been primarily cleaning up the effects of the previous Administration, as President Obama talked openly about, at back yard gatherings among Democrats and Republicans all along. (I had been watching all such broadcasts). As well, giving people SSI benefits and expecting them to invest in the stock market is "crazy", as a number of Senators have been heard to say in recorded Hearings and statements to the press! The whole economy was driven to a form of bankruptcy and economists have told us so. The new administration legislators have no political agenda, but have shown a deep concern to clean up the prevailing problems in America, which have kept them busy day and night in the Senate and Congress for all 18 months- (Again, I have been watching). There are really no agreed upon generic investment places that are considered generically trusted, now, in the sleuth maze of business and banking and investment organizations to "invest" with, as stated by professionals in the market who have been interviewed, as the American people have been informed of the many scandals, to date, and certainly if you don't have enough money to adequately and safely invest, you would not risk it, but every educated American knows this, while private agenda silver-tongued Republicans talked much in the previous administration about pie in the sky ways that privatization could allow the people to *save for their own future*. THAT is a sham— It does not exist, say the Senatorial consensus, while people in big business who want to be free to make all the rules won't care about people who need to get ahead in life who have it tough—They in effect, won't mind controlling outcomes as they have shown themselves to do, and business has taken advantage of others, as we have seen in the top Finance companies, proved in the Senate Committee Hearings, which the taking advantage has been referred to as *business-as-usual*, and what they have shown us in the recent past, for even *over* eight years. Please, let's not be as insulted or demeaned as to think that Americans who have knowledge and wisdom don't realize this! The Economy is progressive, yet still "broken". My goodness, we cannot wave a 'magic wand'! The people listened to the get rich quick method of deregulation and it lead to bankruptcy and a deficit economy! While we do need to think carefully about insurance rates for those with healthcare plans, no question, it is now about those who want money, control and power, versus those who want balance, equity, justice and accountability as well as prosperity, for all people and not just the rich! There are no quick fixes or silver bullets- or magic wands! Those in power, the Democrats, presently know this and kept those who locked THEM out, originally, from pushing through improper legislation on bills that would hinder small business and would assist corporate business, so when they, the Republicans, got power through many tax breaks originally, they wanted to maintain that status, forever, and allow a way of doing business *which does not allow the common person to get a financial foothold in the economy.* It is true that Democrats do not want insurance rates to soar or for people to have insurance problems. They have been working toward that end in helping America. Numerous Hearings on C-span I have watched attest to this fact. Deficits were bequeathed us, from the previous administration, let us not forget. Let us not repeat those mistakes in the near future, and by all means, proceed with caution!

Tax breaks to the wealthiest and legislation to put all of such as that in place, favoring the rich, led to leverage for big business and the Republican platform, as viewed on C-Span broadcasts, and that was when the Republicans decided to lock out the Democrats—(If you watched it all, non-moderated, at the edge of your seat). The Democrats (as I did watch the broadcast on when that took place), were astonished that the Republicans decided at the last minute to go against Constitutional Democracy, and lock out the Democrats, back when they did, and since Democrats have equal rights to assemble and to discuss the bills, Constitutionally, and to vote on them. There should never have been a split in the House of Representatives. Basic Constitutional Democracy is important to uphold, but to maintain *good faith*, essentially when the Republicans did not allow equal assembly in Congress to the Democrats, e.g. (equal right to assemble in the House), constitutionally speaking, so as to block legislation and right to assemble, and input from Democrats, which is un-Constitutional. Fair people allow fair presence and assembly, in an egalitarian manner. Unfair practice of equality- as recently, in the midst of the Salmonella case concerning Hill and Dale Farms repeat violations of safety and cleanliness in other farms they ran, under Presiding Bart Stupak's guidance, where Senator Burgess said that he wanted to mention (*right in the middle of the case*), his Republican agenda on current healthcare filibustering by Senator Coburn, that such filibustering (or holding up the passing of certain bills) was: "to the credit of Republicans", in that also taxes is an issue for those who are seeking their business interests in insurance, and other industries- he had to be stopped by the Hearing leader. So how can one know why these bills are being presently filibustered? It is unlawful to take Hearing floor time to plug a party interest. Burgess yet mentioned that he felt that Coburn should be exempt from personal accountability like other Republicans for filibustering or taking floor time to make political preference statements which is not in keeping with the rules, and unlawful. He claimed that it was not Senator Coburn who was filibustering Congress to not allow taxes to go through for wealthy "responsible" wealthier businessmen, which was incorrect, according to objective media reports and as addressed in rebuttal by Bart Stupak, presiding Hearing officer, regarding Coburn's filibustering or blocking the potential passing of a healthcare bill which would hasten to *lessen* the fiscal tax so-called "burden" on the assumed wealthiest 'players' in the financial/business sectors, some of whose interests might have influenced actions of members of the finance sector who were responsible for faulty derivative loan packages, as has been determined by the Hearings and the Senator leaders who presided in those Hearings, in cross-examinations, recently. To somehow imply as the Majority Party Senators have, that Middleclass America would not receive the lessening of their tax burden, thus the notion, to state that Wealthy America should therefore share in extended tax breaks written into law for them, formerly, which have now technically come to an end, at the end of the old Bush administration.  For over eight years, these tax breaks were extended and  only *now* have now been ended, but by allowing those tax breaks to continue, which now, cannot be maintained *but will be re-legislated due to being at the end of the year's legislative cycle*, Senator Burgess violated the process of the Hearing room rules, did in the midst of an objective case, try to push his personal interest platform at the time of that broadcast over two months ago, and make a plug for the Republican party, was not proper. It is not about Republicans and Democrats!—It is about *Justice and proper ethics in Hearings, and proper business operation, proper balanced taxes and no unequal burden to the middleclass which has been paying all along.* (If you pay attention, and look very closely, and listen attentively) to Congress, Senate, and see how many people are wealthy and follow who they are and their interests, you will also see their agenda come into focus. You can see who owns and has mostly all the wealth and understand why the Republicans want to control the House, in terms of the higher percentage of income and desire greater numbers in the House. Democrats wanted to and have gained house seats. Senator Bird died trying to work and fight toward House equity/fairness, if it be known to society, if you've been watching. It is crisis for Senators to be at each others' throats to establish an era of *just* legislation and business which is *not to the advantage of bureaucrats in Senate who investigate financial and legal flaws—Quite the contrary: for wanting proper regulations and proper Constitutional accountability regarding economic distribution of tax responsibility, after an era of tax relief and prosperity for a division of citizens in highest income bracket of business, who have the highest advantage, bureaucrats who wring their hands, truly want economic balance. Corporate wide*, the statistics show that Corporations have benefitted, and according to the recent radio 88.5 broadcast of the *Divergence statistics reported from Washington D.C. that the wealthiest sector received the* 9% trickle down of those favored legislated breaks, as reported by Economists in Washington D.C.—(who were not reporting in favor of any party, but just doing their job), while 3% trickle down got to the less fortunate small business and poverty sector. This is sort of like <u>Standard and Poor</u>'s statistics, from Wall Street, which is like the standard way of business versus what the poor need, to define what the researchers say in <u>Standard and Poor</u>'s is referring to, in understanding what is going on in business economics, made simple. For me it is easy to understand. Money and power is central to the wealth maintenance strategy agenda, and they don't care how they get or maintain the power, if you watch them in every senate floor lobby, their style in filibustering and blocking bills, using power in numbers, which is typically their style trend, if you watch carefully, which is consistent among Republicans, but Democrats: Their style trend is that they tend to get information, see where the legislative discrepancies are, see the economic difference in the math of business prosperity between one group of people and another, which makes them look slower than Republicans, as they chase down the facts, focus on people and spend their time mostly not on formulating new business *gain* strategies, so much as interstate, regulatory and insurance rate legislation, (of just a few of the needed legislation done on bills), out of fear, currently, not without weighing the consequences to *people*, which tends to be the difference in the parties, if you really have been paying objective attention to the evolution of the actions used to stop the left wing, versus the actions taken to stop the pundit right wing. Rhetoric for *special interest constituency games* and the continued push of the right wing to continue the same tax cuts for the wealthiest people, are part of a continued Republican agenda, while appealing to their right wing colleagues in these floor sessions, and trying to appeal to some democrats, to see if others would go along with them, to gain profits with them, as the Republican campaign styles of special interest which has been termed as part of "business- as- usual" has been admonished as *needing to be changed*, by Democrats and the New Administration, as they are at each other's throats over it. The style of wealthy politics and maintained interests, which Bush asked his cronies if they missed him yet in the Congress and Senate in Washington D.C., sometime ago, then much later, (just recently), Bushes' book about his alcoholism and life came out, and how he did not realize he said, that he was managing the taxpayer's money. That's absurd. Republicans had been still operating in the business- as- usual G.W. style that G.W. Bush had encouraged among Republicans, before refereed by Obama in the referendum- (common knowledge in the News), *as you cannot have tax law reform both ways*. If you benefitted one side of the equation of people, you must in all fairness then benefit the other side of the equation of people (in all fairness) *in terms of tax relief, and in reference to tax "burden".* It is time in other words, to benefit small business now, after Big and corporate business has been so benefitted. That is *sound business economics* concerning *cycles* and *trajectories* which involve *foreign trade, investments*, global small businesses, business development, ERA, Interstate laws and imports, exports, roads, jobs: *public sector* versus *private sector.* By the way, most of the new jobs were created in the *Private Sector* and not the poorer *Public sector,* and wealthier people control the private sector. If you watch and read all the papers which highlight the Republican tendencies to seek to find more ways to justify keeping those same and other similar tax cuts, they seek to shift the tax burden once again, to the small businessman- they continue to do just that, legislatively in filibustering, and in small local laws, which leave the small business man out, then they have accused Obama of potentially trying to charge higher taxes on the Middleclass as he now follows through t*o not allow* Big and Corporate business to continue to receive tax breaks, in Congress and Senate legislation, so the rich try to use a fear tactic on unsuspecting small businessmen who are *'running to catch up'*, in business, as Obama puts it. Wealthy, top-of-the-economic bracket Republicans have been playing this "fat cat" "game" for a long time and know how it is played in business. They have had education, freedom, ease of lifestyle and deregulation on their side for many years, which according to Obama now requires *restrictions*. (Restrictions are simply a normal course of business, and legislation). You will notice who owns the money, the property, the golf courses and whose interests are priority to those with the access to power who have enjoyed that power without disruption, consistently in the last 30 years, if you watch closely and have been paying attention. Do the Historical Political research and follow it before World War I, then to World War II, and the Reagan era, and you will see, in the decline of Democracy since Eisenhower, and after particularly President Kennedy, then Nixon, what occurred in the economy, if you really pay close attention to history, politics, business, economics, and how it works. Then follow it up to the present, after Reagan. And we are not in the same economy as the Reagan years, so the Republican argument about going back to the Reagan years philosophy will not work s we are not in that economy. One has to wonder how valuable the tax breaks extended were for the wealthiest and its impact upon the middleclass back in the Reagan years as a recent documentary merely mentioned that mistakes were made in that management but not enough time to address the full details was a problem in that documentary, as so many details were given about that time period and its complexities. But most Americans don't have that kind of understanding of History and Political Science, nor do they have the time, it seems, and they are unwilling to talk about it, of course. Most Americans don't seem to be educated in such a manner, nor do they seem to have the acquired taste for the love of paying focused attention for hours to committees, speeches, political process, much less the legislative process, as a hobby, in the off hours, unless they have pursued it as a discipline, as one must really have an interest and acumen, as well as the desire to learn the nomenclature for the sake of knowledge in it, law and justice, and fewer people I have encountered in life, seem to have that basic drive, to be honest with you, unless they are in such professions, whom I find refreshing when I find them, socially. But don't take my word for it, find out for yourself. Most people just want to make money and that is the issue in America, today. Mostly persons in government office have demonstrated in numerous C-Span non-moderated broadcasts, in the actual committees, hearings, senate meetings, floor debates and Congress itself, the drive to parse the deeper facts of the issues and legislation, to balance them, and to indeed have the mentality for it, and the concern for it, with no private agenda. No one can use the excuse that television does not do accurate reporting, but television does accurate objective listening in the Hearing and Committee rooms, at least on C-Span, and documentaries, where many sitting around a table eking out the facts separately, trying to get to the bottom of a case, try to piece the case together, if you study the Hearings, which reveals that the committees, Senators, listen to the testimonies of those on trial, for hours and days on end. Read History books, listen to History documentaries, and many committees on television-*just those alone*, if you really listen critically and are not distracted, but watch and compare other speakers and develop a taste for critical *hearing* toward hearing the truth beyond what people say. When you master issues and get the facts piece at a time, for yourself from many sources, then you can parse issues on your own, responsibly. Many citizens can. The privileged got a hold of so much power and wealth, they felt they owned the Whitehouse and America, as the objective facts were revealed in all the Hearings and Committees, to Senate, piece by piece, which sought the truth and to understand what happened in business in America, so the wealthy expected to turn the tide to a Plantation mentality, complete with persons who were laughing at the poor, even laughing at the present administration for having any sense of equality and decency for suffering Americans, if you watched them. I did. The right wing "extremists" come from the premise that *you can build your own future*, when many Americans *don't have enough to build a life, let alone, a future*. While many Republicans in Senate have agreed that there is a rift and a huge gap between the rich and the poor, some Republicans will consistently go so far as to try to have those who do not have proper access to education, believe that *no taxes to the wealthy* private agenda is the right way in seeking to maintain its hold on economics *which actually, in truth, disrupts the fabric of life in business and jobs in the private and public sectors, while taking advantage of power and has led us to a near second Great Depression!* Economics and the study of it is an objective science which is interpreted on the basis of facts and actions associated with business facts, figures, and cycles, legislation and fiscal responsibility, and law, which includes taxes. Money is power. Such people with the most money and power want to rule over the poor and to "create a permanent underclass" as radio station 88.5 had said numerous times in its broadcasts as has CBS radio station also made similar broadcasts in the past. Most busy Americans don't have the time to listen to issues in great detail, so wealthy special interest groups use what people don't know to their own platform advantage, while persons who are more interested in a fair Democracy and equal opportunity, seek to inform and to educate people, most usually, as is their trend if you watch them and listen to them critically, regularly and watch what they do in legislation on the Senate floor and in Congress, and, watch carefully what their motives are. But everyday people are often not even as aware of the economic nomenclature styles used differently by each party in the Senate and Congress and in legislation of bills, as the current President speaks of openly in his administration of all necessary and important changes which effect all sectors as it must be properly executed and faithfully, while reported to the American people, which he has, and in his weekly address to the public as well, broadcasted on T.V. . Taxes upon the wealthy will not *hurt* the wealthy. Local government for our city nearly came to a standstill as did business and business productivity until a certain point after 18 months of new legislation and reform with the new incumbent Presidential administration. I witnessed it personally in my city. It's not rocket science; it is business and legislative science, law and implementation.

We as a Nation need no more unethical, unprincipled raised Costs which forces business toward expense in business and leads to motives that lead to: 1. Demands, or forced or arbitrarily raised Costs which pulls the economy toward inflation, or economic imbalance (over time) in an economy, is seen as the most likely *cause of inflation, by economists*. What tends to lead to the *demand toward inflation* is: 2. Spending *beyond production in business*, (as in the previous Presidential administration) which then led to: 3. Inflation; (and its motivations), (because improper management and planning, without attention to regulation is not technically founded upon sound constitutional principles), which then in turn, led and leads to: 4. Cost increases and greater expenses, in the cost to do business, and retail consumer products prices, which got passed down to consumers, ultimately, *which is where the current Economy is now*, which is the problem-that is, when costs soar, the economy gets out of balance, which all amounts to the huge lack of accountability by special interest private agenda groups whose motive is to get rich quick and to have less attention to regulation, which is associated with good faith practice, in the quality of service that America was once famous for! 5. Cost increases leading to inflation has been determined to be the *main cause of inflation*, according to *economists*. Cost increases and inflation takes place when *the cost to produce rises at a faster rate than a country's production goods output, so the cost of raw materials goes up.* Spending more than you can replenish fast enough, or deficit spending, creates this. The next principle that one needs to watch, as the economy experiences a shift in the economic curve, after costs and inflation, then, goes up, is: 6. A decrease in employment, which becomes part of a process of attempting to lower business costs, to increase productivity and savings, *to make the most of one's profits*. Basically, *if you did not raise prices too soon*, you could *stave off inflation and cost increases*, and obviously if you did not *outsource*, or not quite so much, you could keep your employees and their jobs, and maintain a better output in the Gross Domestic and finally Gross National Product, in the Nation. Not all people have access to the same opportunities, or exact same access to same goods and services, generally, which is why regulation is so *vital to sound* business practice. But in a global world, global competition in goods and services, industry wide, is changing this access. Next: 7. Currency injection: A faster velocity of currency injected into the economy can allow a unit of currency to purchase multiple times its value, in an economy, as President Lincoln did during the time of the Confederacy, as he could not afford to borrow money and also used bonds for the security and *slow growth maturity* of those bonds invested in the Confederacy compact for the war effort. The value of bonds today, is not the same as it was in Lincoln's day. If there is, in a more advanced economy, a greater population and more *aggressive* business practices, which can undermine *sound* economic security, there tends to be a lot of disregard for economic balance, in pursuit of profits, over extended periods of time where a surplus has been spent too rapidly, and with regard to larger growth cycles, followed by lower growth cycles, in a large population, such as we have just experienced in our economy, therefore, large, then small growth, with mu statistical average of significance in populations noted, (concerning economic deficiencies), concerning analyses of progress, and decline, which take place through a specified growth cycle, (after fast growth then slow growth), especially if a surplus gained through the fast growth cycle phase of an economy with a *much larger demographic population*, is *spent more rapidly than replenished* in a *then* slow growth phase. Then, in such an economy, there is a *greater danger of shortfall*. It is like double indemnity, so to speak. It puts the economy in a double-bind and requires quick bail-out measures as the growth rate does not move fast enough, to compensate for the discrepancies created, which leads inevitably, to *shortfall*, while inadequate provision for *added insurance security*, if not provided for in the *treasury*, like *not keeping enough money on hand in the bank when you have many loans taken out in a cycle or period of need in the economy*, creates a *tendency* toward a *shortfall*, coupled with such a looming deficit, due to issues surrounding planning, (or the failure thereof), where a fast growth cycle followed by a slow growth cycle in an economy cannot make up fast enough for the deficit shortfall due to nothing to back up the immediate need for cash in depleted reserves which need to be backed up with *real currency value* and not merely printed money. All printed money needs to be backed up in the treasury by securities. This is where regulation is critical as opportunities are created within the realm of maximum efficiency and proper business planning with proper maintenance, which should create a well maintained surplus. The next principle is that you should not spend up the surplus, but rather, find the best way to maximize profits, with proper investments, to further back securities, to also maximize returns from good faith business to those who thus return the good faith, theoretically, in your service and work, and good investment strategies, (including adjusting foreign trade duties), create true security and not the opposite, which is created with too much borrowing and non-backed lending. The way to do this is to not over lend without backing it up, and not to neglect the needs of those in true need of good products or service and to retain good employees, products and investments. As well as to not frustrate the disadvantaged or to try to make him pay more than he can reasonably afford and still afford food, is crucial, as not all persons have exact access to education and economic security or adequate wages. Greed can have the effect of quashing good faith relationships and will in turn tend to destroy your bottom line. In society, I tend to find more often than not, by way of another example, that the privileged have not gotten back to me where it concerns the need for closure in communication concerning major issues having to do with services and good faith, and where life demands some deep analysis and understanding of circumstances, and with my having given very specific follow-through (on my part), I have tended to find that persons who are not acquainted with human need really don't seem to be sympathetic to the needs I am experiencing, and that they essentially don't feel they have to be, I have found, therefore, I have been neglected in some cases repeatedly, due to challenges beyond my control and often the lack of quality control has ensued, when I have been extremely patient, both as a consumer and a manager- also as a consultant, and have been *welcoming* to those who don't offer the same, but tend to expect my sympathy and understanding as well as support, regardless. They too often have told me there was nothing they could do to help me, or to work favorably with me, when years before the privileged agenda took over; there was at least accountability and at least, a sense of fair, sound Democracy and concern. Democracy has much to do with fairness and fair play in an egalitarian society—and with regard to self interest—that is as Shakespeare might have said: "much ado about nothing" so to speak, or in the final analysis, in business, that is, it amounts to nothing or *no help*, I have found. Ask anyone in business. It is no less than *lack of accountability and concern*, in *having power* that tends to challenge business and the bottom line, which as President Madison said: *"Absolute power corrupts absolutely"—that's constitutional and not surprisingly so, that it was written by a forefather who was concerned about service and proper use of power.* We've seen this before. If it were not true in his day, he would not have said it, and as a rule, it has always been true of those who get more access to money... Money is power. It changes people. The more they have, the more freedom they also have, and often, the less they tend to care, these days about others' rights, health, safety, well-being or prosperity, as we have seen, everywhere in society. THAT requires more regulation, NOT LESS. Please let us not fool ourselves on that point. It is very *obvious*. Loyalty is the issue here, and concern, which is *good faith*. One does not have to question those who cater to special interest and think endlessly of how much more they can charge without any regard for those in society who cannot afford the cost of living nor have access to opportunities in business and education—THAT is simply not regulated and unjust, and *should* be obvious to any *thinking* citizen who is interested in the preservation of life or equality and fair play, in *any* society of concern. THAT is not a "left wing" notion. THAT is a JUST notion. I consider myself to be a Progressive, but tend toward Democracy and Democratic Justice, by critical listening and participation in listening to the whole Senate debate and floor, finding myself generally legally siding with the balanced wisdom of the Democratic bills for practicality, with some Republican tendencies as well on some bills— it depends upon what the issues are and who those bills benefit and which Republican is proposing them and for what issue, in that I tend to find per legislated bill that I tend toward fair Democracy which is usually demonstrated by persons *who care about others first*, and then *seek economic gain, second*, legislated well by a Democratic or *Democracy* mentality, (*lately*), and some (but very few) Republicans, or Republic mentalities, by those of us who love the Republic or group of those committed to living rightly and well, in a compact, as in the first *Declaration of Independence and Constitutional compact, which was* created by our forefathers, *for and by the People*, but mostly I've tended to see on the Senate floor and Congress that *Republicans* lately tend toward their special interests and colleagues' interests for their overall special interest which is where it is going today, if you watch the debates for hours, objectively. It just has turned out that way. I form my opinions based upon the balanced actions *or* the *restricting of opportunity from bad legislation that has kept me from procuring what I need in the economy, and the normal economics flow of jobs and access on the internet,* which has picked up in 18 months after gridlock, with the installment of the new Presidential administration, to be honest— Otherwise I would have no strong opinions where justice is concerned. I do things based upon *proof* and *issues voted upon* and *legislated* along with *examining issues* and *why people do what they do and who opposes and why.* THAT is how I am motivated- those are my motivations. It does not bother me that my way of analyzing is not like some other citizens, because these days, I find citizens tend to get easily stressed, confused on issues, (not necessarily their fault always), and they may not be certain whom to believe, they react and sometimes don't listen, and sometimes don't allow someone's view and can force their opinions which makes me feel threatened, and *I want to hear it from the legislators* and *not second hand, which I don't listen second hand, anyway.* I realize that people are upset and trying to understand. If I hear reports, I watch the legislation and listen carefully to those who give an objective report and allow *all* viewpoints, to weigh in carefully, *all* the facts and matters concerning general economics, before I make a well-informed decision-- THAT takes a lot of critical listening and thinking in a non-biased fashion. I vote the same objective deliberative way on every topic and proposition. I like to be literate and think for myself, and to know for certain what I should do. I do have opinions as most educated or curious people do, but I am *very objective* in my listening, essentially. I wish more people were. I love law and the legislative process, however arduous it may be—it is interesting. People are impatient and fail to understand economics, legislation and tax cuts in that they fail to watch legislation which would tell them many answers to their questions.

They don't watch Senate and the legislative process, most of them don't unfortunately- THAT is the problem. If you notice, taxes on items you purchase in the general market, say at Walgreens or Office Depot, and on water, and bathroom tissue, and mouthwash, the local business and government has been quietly and steadily increasing the taxes over time, and the tax rate has been raised and adjusted twice in two years, per precinct and district, if you pay attention to those kinds of facts- even the cost of stamps, if you have been paying attention. Local government and business does that, *not your big government.* These are the people *locally* who have the money and power. If you reflect on the billions of people there are in the world, it is not hard to see how they come up with more revenues, and "flat tax", *however, that won't be enough to solve the problems. Besides, the little people are already nickled and dimed to death!* – THAT is why it is wise to look closely at the fine print! *We will need taxes on the richest and the rich cannot be exempt as they would like to be which Bush was trying to do for them and himself endlessly- to create a buddy rich network so that he could pat them on the back and have easy business and make it all so easy for everyone who has money, but business does not work that way. It never has in American History. Special interest is special interest- That is what it means: It is an interest in one's self alone- self aggrandizement. Governance means to look after and to manage the whole of society, and to do it well. It is not popular, but it is important to do.*

The Financial Sector tells us, Christopher Dodd and Barney Frank legislation, particularly Chris Dodd tells us Finance, was: "unregulated all together" and that we have to establish a comprehensive framework and have those who do the financials work and those who "interpret the law" "—that is the Constitutional burden if you live in America. If you don't want to live in America, you are free to go and live in another country—perhaps a dictatorship, if you prefer. Dodd realized how scary "unregulated" was. "Mark my words"... He continued, with the new legislation at the Hearing, "there will be another crisis" he admonished as he said they were setting down laws to regulate business, which is the proof that for too long no regulations were applied to deal with the harsh economic realities and stunted economic growth literally caused by greedy unregulated businessmen which up until the last 18 months nobody could really talk about in the mass society. How scandalous- which of course set about the Dodd/Frank bill legislation, to correct the Federal Reserve problems, the Banks, the Finance companies concerning derivatives and insurance and Real Estate and loan transactions, in their oversight legislation for the purpose of implementing new Financial Regulations in the Senate Banking Committee. Senator Dodd is a Democrat from Connecticut and is financially, legislatively and politically adept as well as quite practical and just in his conduct in Hearings and the legislative process I have witnessed, in hours of his working with other Senators who are Democrat and Republican. At first many people laughed at Barney Frank, but later, he was applauded by intellectuals and top businessmen and their colleagues. No ONE party ever does these Hearings ALONE, and each representative DOES HIS listening and asking of questions separately and objectively, in that first, they have to get the facts. People need FACTS, not what they WANT to BELIEVE. Here are more facts for you: Even discussions with Chairman Bernanke of the Banking Industry and Treasury proved to be frustrating in that Bernanke did not seem to want to regulate when he clearly should have as the Senate representatives had determined in their findings. Bernanke felt the Banks should do as they felt necessary for the sake of business, as everyone felt the industry was "too big to fail" and allowed too many unregulated loans to pass without superior ratings which they were reported by the finance companies to actually have, such as double and triple A ratings which were *misnomers* and were thus, *fraud*, it was brought to light.  It was discovered by Hearing Committee Senators, in Hearings, painstakingly, that No one can write up insurance to back such derivatives since it is illegal and cannot be used in the fashion it was used, in numerous loans, as the Senate representatives indicated in the Hearings, chiefly Senator Dodd, nor such expensive loans, that were not regulated nor watched for pay-out, per month, as elaborated upon in the Hearing, to make sure companies didn't try to add fees at will, or cheat on the pay out to the insurance or mortgage company, by changing the rules, but few if any of these charlatans were actually made to fully account for their deeds as more ponzi schemes were discovered one by one, and the loans were approved apparently by a well known ratings company for the major Financial company players which looks like obvious fiscal awareness of those who transacted the loans, as determined by the Hearing representatives, when you look at the nature of this kind of business. No one can sanction an A or AA rating or AAA rating without legal documentation and these companies just did not have it!- They defrauded the public as the Hearing Committee representatives indicated, and caused persons to have to pay additional unsanctioned loan amounts or not be able to pay off the loans they took out when the financiers ought to have already qualified the validity of these loans and whether or not, persons would be able to make good on those loans for the sake of being backed by banks and insured for such large transactions which those who did the business did so not in good faith, therefore, and endangered the public, so they could get rich quick, which is what was indicated in the Washington D.C. Hearings that took place regarding where the unregulated business problems took place. What was important was to adequately qualify loans, and to make certain that the loans, long term, were doable, which was part of *legislated standards* and authority as a large number of persons were held in Hearings as *Financial Fiscal representatives* were reported by Senate Representation: Dodd, Frank and Waxman, to have inadequately represented the public, not to mention the persons who took out some loans to buy homes, made connections which were in some cases, quick arrangements which were hastily performed. Some purchases were not prequalified well, according to Senate Hearing authorities in some cases, as determined by Senate representatives in accordance with legal standards preset in Finance, concerning credit and spending practice, and regulation, as is reported in the Dodd Frank Hearings. In some cases it was determined that some people had made deals with persons they thought they knew, short order, because that is how the business trends were going, and with that were working within an unstable business market which was fraught with stress as it was, but that was just the finance sector. The Same Senators noted that the same kind of schemes was being applied to education in schools across the country, later. So much was out of balance during and after the Dot com years, and thereafter, then the $787 Billion Dollar Bailout hit. Regulatory agencies admitted in the Hearings they were not keeping track of some regulations and loans to the extent that they were processing more of them and attentive to less regulatory functions, for which they were further questioned, while it was determined by the Senators that fiscal demands became higher then capital reserves kept on hand, again, mentioned in those Senate Committee Hearings on C-Span. Likewise in the Securities regulation end of business, another spokesperson was questioned later as to why regulation concerning the paperwork in certain derivative and loan transactions were processed the way they were which was determined to contribute to loan questions Mr. Dodd sought to understand in greater detail. (After the first set of hearings)—(if you watched them), and with that, a second set of Hearings were held wherein spokespersons were held accountable later and questioned to provide more detailed information on practices concerning millions of dollars which were under scrutiny of Senator Dodd and Senator Frank. The Hearing Representatives were visibly stunned and shocked about information they heard. Spokespersons were reticent to give details and too often declined to do so, thereafter. Originally, Senator Dodd and his panel had had a status quo and "do as you see fit" mentality, in the first Hearing. Later, details came out in the Hearings which followed the first. But government people seemed to have little affiliation with the fiscal protocol and processes in the financial and regulatory sectors, and nomenclature as well, because they work in government and Congress has its own nomenclature, work, and practices, as well as amendments they have had to hammer out. There is a gap in communication and understanding between these branches of service. The best way to encourage right behavior when you are in any professional service is to set good examples, or else people have a tendency not to trust your words in connection with your actions and those with power tend to favor their agenda. Regulatory agencies and requisite "subsidiary" organizations linked to them were under scrutiny.

A decade before all of this trajectory in conflict zones became a high priority issue, and, before Saddam Hussein started to become out of control, as a dictator of sorts, in the Middle East, the consciousness level of terrorism was not part of the American consciousness, and business had not reached its limits to the rainbow's end, shall one say... regarding business, commerce, peace and freedom in countries and across the lines of Nations and countries, onto business boundaries, the trajectories of conflicts in business seemed to be heated to the point of ready for the forging of difference among philosophy and priority among Corporation and Country interest, which came in various sizes, shapes, forms and flavors. Western influence and wealth should not be underestimated in foreign countries or at home, and as we see, the now Secretary of State, Hillary Clinton, has her plate full, in seeking peace in the Middle East while business seeks its mutual interest toward prosperity. If this pursuit of prosperity is merely for those tope 10% who have had freedom and access with little accountability for 8 years, as reported in numerous media broadcasts and channels, on the radio and in the News, then one can imagine the effects, as those who hold greater responsibility are also the *more accountable* for global example and integrity which is translated as I understand American's Constitution, as part of the "domestic tranquility", and "the general welfare", or at least, what contributes to it, in any society. A Nation's wealth-makers, so to speak, under the Constitution of the United States, are representatives of America to other countries. The philosophy or notion of Economic Representation seems to work best, in business practice, performed in a bilateral manner, if you will, and not a unilateral one, which is to say that general Democracy and NOT Autocracy, certainly not Oligarchy, seems to maintain democratic prosperity and economic balance for peoples, to provide a balanced, healthy and civil society, as we have seen after Colonization, within the provisions *The Declaration of Independence*, of the United States of America, and the statutes of *The Constitution*, in American History, particularly. As well, a firm grasp on management, or matching populations to resources and not overusing precious resources, seems to be a wise use of power, as resources tend to grow scarce over time, which is equally important to keep in mind, with an increasing population. Everything is *math*—which is part of *Economics*. To ignore the precepts of prosperity and numbers, and what shapes it, is by definition, a property of *improper management*, which is what life comes down to: Management—regarding local and global efforts, no matter what rhetoric people may immerse themselves in, ultimately. Business is about common sense and right management, and increasingly so in a growing world population, with shrinking resources. Ignoring these precepts creates a double-standard in America, in a bi-Partisan way, leading to crossroads of every kind. Americans should therefore not be amazed at rifts in social peace. We can see this where German Unity is such a high priority in Bremen and Berlin in business and social and governmental politics today. Finland leads in excellence and intelligence in Global education, while the United States ranks a low 17th in math and science now in 2010, according to European broadcast news.

More facts on oil, foreign trade, the economy, clues about business and how it is conducted globally came to light in another interesting case account, in a Hearing when recently, a terrorist case which formerly had been legislated and sent through due-process came up in the News once again when The Pan American flight 1-3 Lockerbie Scotland terrorist bomber was set free, March 5th, 2010 with a transfer written to send the terrorist back to Libya by the Scottish government as a terrorist al-Megrahi, a terrorist bomber, was recently set free and sent back to Libya, after being convicted of 270 counts of murder in his act of the bombing of the Pan Am plane. British Petroleum negotiated the release of the terrorist. David Miliband, British Foreign secretary, said publically, that business could be damaged in Britain and Scotland, should the terrorist remain on Scottish soil, and due to the terrorist developing prostate cancer. The Principal Deputy Assistant Secretary of State Bureau of European Affairs was present in the Hearings which reviewed the medical records and advice, as well as the mandates that the terrorist serve out his sentence in Scotland due to the serious nature of his crimes and government sanctions concerning such cases. The American people were under just legislation to receive nothing less than such justice. Federal Regulation leaders admonished that the terrorist should serve out his term, which indeed one of the family members of flight I-3, wrote a letter which shared the grief concerning the sentence not being carried out for the atrocity the terrorist planned out, as did many other family members who wrote similar letters, which then in his release due to compassion for the terrorist's cancer, on the part of the British government was considered by the regulatory spokespersons as not fulfilling justice. The Scottish authorities considered that the terrorist be granted the compassionate release, as well, BP concluded that it would be in the financial best interest of Britain, Scotland and Libya to have the prisoner returned. Apparently, Scotland was to stand to gain oil for the release of the prisoner and Britain millions. The United Kingdom made the decision to change their agreement with the U.S. over the incident, but privately, without informing the U.S. in what was politically elitist and considered by Senate members in the Hearing to be improper as U.S. courts indicate. It was determined that only Judicial concerns would be considered originally, in fact, and NOT economic concerns, in the British government in the first agreement between the countries. Perhaps what was implied was the damage that could happen to any kind of business in England or Scotland, in being closer to the Middle East than the U.S. it appears, as seeming fear in housing the prisoner on Scottish soil might have been partly a motivation to send him back to Libya. It looks more like a diplomatic attempt at maintain safety and peace under the category of "compassionate release" given the unrest of Libya and the terrorism which is close proximity to Scotland and England. But it could have actually been a decisive preference for business and economic interest, solely, which could obstruct justice, (or a combination of the motivations mentioned). It is hard to tell, but this situation gives you a glimpse at foreign affairs and business and how difficult it is to govern these issues, as well, how they affect business. The Foreign policy ministers completed the transfer to release the prisoner when all political leaders in all countries had agreed it was important for all parties' interests that the terrorist serve out his sentence in Scotland, originally. The only other reason was that his body was deteriorating and great bone degeneration with the disease having spread through the body as stated by Medical professionals. The person received chemotherapy however, which was documented, to reduce pain, and create longevity. Through hormone therapy and radiation the person was treated with success for the pain and disease, as the hormones were treated and problems had come from the adrenal glands, it was determined by Medical officials. The terrorist was reported not to receive treatment and yet the Doctor in Chief contends that the man would have received the treatment in order to still be living today and to be standing and released walking, as he was, which the terrorist is still living, therefore. He had been required to live out his sentence in Scotland, in prison. This was an anomaly situation apparently. The question becomes who wanted the terrorist to return to Libya, for what reason and why and how was he released? How will this impact life, business and economics as well as the foreign affairs of State? Why then as Foreign Affairs Miliband stated, would imprisonment *"not be good for business"?* According to the foreign affairs and the British government, what relation has this to do with BP oil? *Whose interest is being served, and why?,* is ultimately the question that Senators were asking in that Hearing, as we in the U.S. have witnessed some other oil dealings in business in other lands while the Nation has sought to be less dependent upon foreign oil, and we have concerns about the way America does business and the war, as well as foreign affairs. Originally a Doctor stated that the terrorist had 3 months to live, in his prognosis, which in fact was not the case and a panel of three doctors determined that in receiving the treatments the terrorist received, (which would have been common medical knowledge they contend,): that the terrorist would have recovered, in their expert diagnostic chief experience, and clinical opinions, which suggests some sort of misaligned medical and diagnostic facts. The question becomes how was information misaligned so the terrorist was sent back, out of supposed "compassion" for his "apparent imminent prognosis of death in 3 months"?, which is what the Senators were grappling with. It is suggested that someone knew and it is suggested most likely that the physicians who treated the terrorist in fact felt he was moving closer to health, so released him under the prognosis of death in 3 months, but that their prognosis was not correct, it was determined, by the Hearing leader. One would have to wonder why this incident occurred in such a manner and why the U.K., for business purposes, let the prisoner go. Anyway, the European secretary of state illuminated that therefore the man should return to fulfill his sentence since he appeared to be healing and moving toward recovery and quite able to stand, where he had not been able to do so many months before the completion of the treatments. The regulatory agencies would have to be checked to see the details of what government officials had done and why they had decided to do what they did in this case. The presiding Senator was the Foreign Relations Committee Acting Hearing Chairman in the Hearing on 9/10/2010 on C-Span. *Oil was clearly on the bargaining table and the securing of those assets in Libya, with millions of dollars to the U.K.* One has to wonder how involved this situation was or if it really was as simple as the U.K. gaining money for its economy which encouraged bi-lateral negotiations. As it was, BP arrangements, to deliver and step up oil production, had issues regarding safety standards, which then led to the BP spill as the Foreign Relations Committee presiding Senator, over the terrorist Hearing, had also presided over the BP spill as well. BP is still in review. Attentiveness is the issue being discussed at present in the Hearings which remain. The greater company share negotiated would have stepped up production and expectations for the business transaction to deliver and make good to Libya, for business or for debts, perhaps most likely, millions to Britain simply, just all that money for business to U.K., or, whichever, and solved the debt problems in financial and public sectors which are similar to the U.S., that the U.K. has, if you watch BBC broadcasts—This sounds plausible: in order to achieve its Foreign Affairs goals, and perhaps U.K. were happy to send back the terrorist so they would not have him on their soil, as well as to make a profit, which is what perhaps could have happened, (but that is speculation). Still, such actions demonstrate once again, that justice and deregulation when paired: *deregulation always seems to win in favor of the profit motive, which is a common theme in the business-as-usual trend, in the U.S., the U.K., Greece, Germany and other Global economies, if you examine how they have similar economic accountability challenges, in all the same ways, in their financial crises and structures, in the trickle down, between the rich and the poor, if you listen and pay attention.* All the countries share the same kinds of shortages and problems in the same sectors of business- Not a coincidence. The coincidence of these crises is just TOO coincidental. It seems we live in the age of get rich quick and not think about the consequences, in favor of a quick profit, which does harm to peoples' lives, which seems a huge issue in all markets, these days, globally. Agreements and safety, the lives of citizens then seem more at risk and as such, safety for citizens seems largely compromised. Business in the Global Markets is much more than just business in America or in just the U.K. as *these markets find themselves increasingly linked and dependent upon one another, more foreign agreements for taxes and duties, and countries choose whom they want to buy from in an increasingly changing and narrowing market structure, due to outsourcing and management expansion. Agribusiness and Chinese goods are an issue of course, as well as other governments being accountable for their actions, involving their currency, goods and services, imports and exports.* This is why America tends to want to support local farms, strongly as well. With a growing population, that too, is a difficult task, along with the costs of food and production and persons wanting a higher wage and to make their "lion's share" of profits as well as in agribusiness. This too has frightening consequences and resources in global warming, in what is a vulnerable economy, in terms of sustaining what America requires, and affordability in shrinking resources. Population growth and global warming are other important issues to consider as the planet is reaching a tipping point. We can't manufacture rain, or feed a growing population without it.

Democrat Senator Debbie Wasserman Schultz, who worked on the Senate and Court Committee Hearings and Trials on Healthcare; The $787 Billion Dollar Bail Out; and other important House and Senate as well as Congressional case rulings, on countless legislative cases I watched for many hours and weeks in 2009-10 on C-Span, was on C-Span, today: October 6th, 2010 telling the American public that from her Congressional experience and Senate floor, watching legislation and being present in Congressional and Financial Hearings for justice in many committee Hearings, that the goal of the Democratic Congress is "not to rob the Republicans of their tax breaks", but in being a Progressive, she asserts that the Democrats' plan is to allow the Middleclass to have their fair share, in reform, of tax cuts or to lessen the burden, so that the Wealthiest Americans can take up their share of the tax burden, now that their tax breaks are coming to an end under the former Bush legislation- Only now, coming due. In essence, the timeline of Washington D.C. political process, is different from the timeline of the business world, of Wall Street and that of the average American citizen, who all live in different timelines in their time zones, if you will, in their respective milieus, wherein each type of citizen observes the political and legislative process, not fully aware of these differing timelines, in their busy lives. Mr. Boehner had made claims that the Republicans intend to win the House and Congress, as yet, Ms. Wasserman Schultz asserts professionally that as such, there is no indication that that ambition will be realized in that the percentages of disappointed Americans is still higher within the Democratic communities, such that the Democrats seem to be winning the campaigns, she announced, locally and in Washington D.C. due to the deficit created by the Republicans, she contends, and that the American people are still very upset by this fact, that the intent of the present body of Democrats is to correct the deficit difficulties as they have started to and to preserve and encourage the right of the Middleclass to receive their fair share of tax cuts, to relieve the burden upon them and to ask the Republicans to take up their fair share of those burdens according to the Constitution. The war will cost well over three trillion she does agree, with the caller who calls in to enter the fray and debate. The issue is about the common defense, regarding that the house seems to be held hostage by the Republican Senators, which Ms. Wasserman Schultz agrees regarding the fact that she states that Republican senators have "filibustered nearly every bill to stop the new legislation" to keep from assisting the Middleclass, and from allowing legislation on their behalf for their *tax* relief "from going through"... while Mr. Boehner says just the opposite to the Tea Party people, while he has been cited as not paying taxes, as part of the top 10% regarding his "golf courses" and other property issues as C-Span Newspaper stories in writing were brought before the cameras, recently to point out on C-Span 1. Boehner is a big speaker currently, as I did witness, seeing the report on C-Span 1, and his golf courses where he spent a lot of time for which "no property taxes" have been paid as the newspaper article was shown on camera close-up. Tighter regulations and the incentivizing for people to do business at home and to generate some responsibility to tax the overseas outsourcing tendency and to de-incentivize it, was a law put into legislation by responsible legislators, most of whom by the way happened to be Democrats, she reveals, in tax law, which Obama she says "delivered tax relief" in his incentivizing to "small business", to undo the Bush tax laws which allow the former recipients of the business privileges to do business and have tax relief , which if you pay attention to the actual businesses and foreign trade as well as manufacturing facts, has been to the benefit of most Republicans who still argued for more desired tax relief, due to the original legislation of deregulation, to allow them to do business as they desired, for all of these years and especially the last eight, which caused the Republicans to believe that business, possibilities in business, and the banks were *"too big to fail".* Who was paying attention to that reasoning? Ms. Wasserman Schultz fears if the tax incentives for the smaller businessman and de-incentivizing business overseas, to bring jobs back to America is not maintained, as Obama said is *necessary,*-(that IS what HE did and is doing), that America will have a harder time of recovery from this recession- which is a valid fear. The next caller mentions that President Obama had "nothing to work with" when he came into office, as Wasserman Schultz contends, "He literally had to rescue it from the jaws of almost another great depression", "we had to rescue them, those businesses, otherwise they would have gone off a cliff"… these are the small businessmen we are talking about, let's understand, as she had reviewed the legal and financial documents of the Billion Dollar Bail Out, was present during the WTO: World Trade Organization meetings, and Homeland Security as well as the general SEC and Treasury Hearings and with Barney Frank during those Hearings regarding also Paulsen and Cashcari, and those who were the spokespersons for the Financial groups represented, along with the SEC, Treasury, and the Banks, Bernanke, regarding the activities of reportedly: Lehman, AIG and Goldman Sachs, and the false double A and triple A ratings leading to derivatives faulty loans, and insurance backed mortgages which led to poorly written and badly executed, non supervised activity on the loans, financials documents, and so-called loan schedules which were further, added to (unlawfully, says Senate Representation), for profit, adding "false charges" even, stated in the Hearings, by Senators Jud Gregg and Senator Kyle, at great length, after the Presidential election and into the quick proceedings of much needed investigation, which was not a priority under the Bush administration under the business-as-usual trend in the previous administration. I recall in watching all of these and other Hearings from back to back, from beginning to end with all the details, for hours and continued into following days of broadcasts, as they extended beyond one and two days, as I recall, in the reporting on television. Reported digit increases at that time, before the Hearings, those digits increasing in insurance premiums, in other Hearings as well, on C-span, before the Obama administration sought to regulate Insurance to make healthcare more affordable to Americans, to make sustainable, the means of provision- little at a time, to regulate and begin that process for needy Americans, which the business sector and Republicans tried to filibuster since the inception of the idea, arguing that business should not be regulated, and that free enterprise, unregulated, would work, which over time has not proved correct, but rather that businesses have taken advantage of clients including well known insurance companies, as they raised their rates, as mentioned in the Hearings, at length, did not provide the services paid for by the clients, then caused the clients to get heart disease and worsening symptoms, as the overall rates for membership were thus also increased, with the excuse of making improvements to the system which the Hearing judge Senator Waxman claimed the insurance company was "padding" its books to the detriment of an "over-percentage" they could not justify in their margin, to the client or to the courts, in that Hearing held over four months ago now. Premiums tend to go up as a rule in Insurance as it is, so require regulation in that type of business. I have finished studies in Insurance, including dividends, which are not taxed presently in corporate shares, or insurance to shareholders. Adding insurance to back mortgages in the way that a particular insurance company did, as reported in the Hearing, was not sanctioned in that they backed the mortgages falsely with surplus they did not have, and that insurance strategy was not necessary, but excessive in those transactions said the Senators in their estimation, after a thorough study of the practices which took place, which in a form, was improper business practice, they concluded. You cannot back what you cannot secure in insurance, otherwise you are leaving in an unstable situation, those who have paid to you the money for their own insurance, if you fail to back up the premiums they have paid to you. One must be able to back the insurance they claim they can provide, first, so essentially, insurance companies did more business than they could back, and in essence, THAT is NOT ethical in the insurance industry, if you study insurance. That's one issue point. Holding the Middleclass as "hostage" and keeping them from realizing their due tax breaks from Constitutional burden is unconstitutional, as a second issue point, IF the Republicans claim to the public that in fact Obama is depriving them of relief, and cause overwhelming healthcare costs, which in fact if monitored, as insurance is now being regulated, can be facilitated with the proper tax adjustment to the appropriate business persons and earning level cap, done proportionately, correctly for large businesses, starting with the incentives of encouraging business and tax breaks for the small businessman to do business locally, which Obama has provided for at present, then it is possible to assume that the healthcare strategy he proposed may work. The slogan of the Republican or repealing the Obamacare agenda, to rationalize not paying taxes is a fear tactic, as stated by Democrats, that Republicans use, to not pay their fair share of taxes, to avoid their tax responsibility, by trying to intimidate the small businessman by telling him that if Obama takes away the big businessman's tax breaks that Obama will surely try to also make the small business man pay those taxes the wealthiest are destined to pay in the new legislation, which Obama has continued to say that he does not approve of one party taking "hostage" the middleclass and would certainly not intend to tax the small businessman who needs to catch up! The Republicans try to scare the small businessman with this view; too, in this hostage game strategy the big businessmen in Washington D.C. keep playing to avoid paying their fair share of taxes. Republicans keep pushing the platform of just let everyone pay their fair share, but no new taxes for big business who they contend grow the jobs, then they can discuss the other items later is their new administrative approach, which stalls their tax responsibility after the tax breaks which are to an end only now, in the present legislation which refers to the top earners of 200k to 250K plus, earners, who are the targeted group, are on the legislative agenda to pay, according to the legislation rules, who have not yet paid their fair share, who must, so that constitutional economic stabilization has a chance to take place in this country, according to the Democrats and President Obama. The small businessman can only seem to see, from review of campaigns and responses to the platforms, how much money he has and has made. He does not seem to know how much more the richer man has in all this activity of "just catching up" as Obama repeatedly says, as I have noted and watched in the statistics. Trade is a matter of writing the rules so that Big Business, Corporate Interests and China will pay taxes, duties and excises, fairly, play by the global rules like everyone else, as America has perfected other sectors of its products other than cars, so that America can feel upgraded in its imports taxes, and across export lines, as China has so many good products, such duties for American products have been overlooked during the Bush administration, according to reports updates, for those of us who have been watching this entire time. One has to see how many good American products there are and to catch up to China in the business practices with G20 and the WTO. This lack of attentiveness along with allowing less tax accountability to the privileged, hurt Main street and Wall street (if you were watching, closely), as did the *outsourcing*, which now *outsourcing* is being taxed for the wealthy business owner to pay his fair share, and to provide more *incentives* for the small local businessman to invest and do business *locally*, at home, which stimulates job growth, according to President Obama. These amendments were a first attempt at establishing a business economic and trade balance, in America, after runaway business produced the $787 Billion Dollar Bail Out, due to negligence in the Financial and Regulatory sectors, as reported in Senate Hearings on C-Span. It is the local businessman and particularly the small businessman whom the large businessman has allowed to carry the tax burden while he has soft-peddled his tax breaks, as reported in the Hearings, and update reports, on C-span, along with the need to attend to duties to

American imports and the Exports issue concerning China , while allowing the outsourcing, the tax benefits and no legislation of outsourcing all this time, the *profits* of it,  and not allowing regulation, while not addressing the legislative *need* to change the *outsourcing business-as-usual practice*, all of this time, *before the new Obama legislation which just took place, so as now, to to relieve the small businessman, with the new Obama legislation. The new administration makes clear to big business that the small local businessman is now being relieved of taxes to keep business at home, in the face of the many needs of employees and rising healthcare costs among the disadvantaged.* The Democratic plan to keep healthcare costs low came from the Democrats, who proposed that far too many Americans were being cheated of services they were paying for in healthcare, or fees were being continually raised on them, or worse, many Americans were not able to afford insurance at all, as stated in updates reports and Hearings on C-span, in the formerly unchecked insurance industry. Let's not forget that managing well and proper taxation is akin to balanced leadership which is fair, practiced in good faith, fairness, and as we have seen demonstrated in Colonial history, is how our Nation became a Nation governed by a *Constitution*, under a *Declaration of Independence*. While religion does not necessarily allow for sound governance in American History, neither from the battlefields nor the Vatican, (if you arduously check the history), and because America's laws and religion *separate church and state*, essentially, in America, *"the land of the free and the home of the brave"*, as sung in our famous anthem, (which is not just Protestant, Presbyterian, or Baptist, let alone Seventh Day Adventist or Methodist, exclusively), one must understand that the Nation was founded upon *sound principles of proper teaching of God and more importantly, good faith in business, but not Religion per se*, if you check European, American and World History, carefully. While I don't consider myself to be Religious, but rather, Spiritual, it is true that William Penn said: "Those who will not be ruled by God, will be ruled by tyrants", and he was not talking about churches ruling people, with special interest or with endless corporate tax relief, for private agendas in business, while ignoring those at the disadvantage, (quite the contrary), but rather, that *where the principles associated* with fair and good faith business practice are not applied to business practices or even sound practice of Religion in any context, universally, (and where compassion and doing unto others as you would have them do unto you is not done), there tends to be a *trend* toward *dictatorship* or *tyrannical leadership* in *one form* or *another*- in *business or religion, which is what William Penn was suggesting.* Let us also not forget that Jesus Himself said, concerning law and not *Religious Doctrine,* regarding doing what one knows is right in business, (*non-hypocritically,*): "For it is not those who hear the law who are righteous in God's sight, but it is those who obey the law who will be declared righteous." (Romans 2:13). Jesus also said concerning the deeds of people: *"figs are not gathered from thorn bushes, nor are grapes picked from a bramble bush. The good person out of the good treasure of his heart produces good, and the evil person out of his evil treasure produces evil"*(Luke 6:44), and in another translation of the Bible it says concerning the same passage, about deeds, done one to another, Jesus went on to say in the same passage: *"you shall know them by their deeds"*, as well He also said: *"because the carnal mind is enmity against God; for it is not subject to the law of God, neither can it be."* (Romans 8:7). In just one more passage concerning paying taxes, Jesus told the Pharisees the following: "render to Caesar the things that are Caesar's, and to God the things that are God's." (Matthew 22:21). Our system of law was built upon God and the Bible and with time, laws emerged which were based upon seeing to balance and fairness among people in villages, from roughly 1200 A.D. and respectively 1300 A.D. as studied in my Case Law courses, to prevent theft, homelessness, the burning of villages and abuse of laborers in common labor and concerning their wages. Laws and Constitutionality, good faith and fairness are about paying one's fair share, constitutionally speaking, which has nothing to do with science and the universe, incidentally, and Democratically speaking. It is more of a moral issue and financial, as well as an economic balance issue. It has nothing to do with space and science, as scientists seem to suggest in modernity regarding religion. Rules evolved out of the logic of a sense of justice, because the laws of justice and concept of not doing to someone what you would not want them to do to you, is just logical. Balance in the economy, is synonymous with justice and fiscal balance, whether it was in the society of the Greeks, whose kingdoms were plagued with Tyrants and eventually fell, or as kingdoms eventually evolved to Colonialism and then to the American *Declaration of Independence* of 1776, which gave rise to our free enterprise system and business structure as we know it, which has worked for hundreds of years. Taxes were charged, more specifically more evenly after Lincoln declared and created the Confederacy Compact, later, after he injected more currency into the weakened economy, and made provisions for slaves to be granted their freedom and right to earn, to be educated and later, therefore, to own. Equal and fair taxes are charged so that life is fair and offers opportunity for everyone so that wealth does not become represented in Oligarchy or Tyranny rule over a Nation. This is why proper taxation and duties as well, in foreign trade, and fair market reports of true value of currency is also part of good faith in trade and business. Next, China is currently informed in our global market, (if you have been watching), that America needs amendments to duties on imports and exports or foreign trade, which involves the WTO: World Trade Organization, and foreign economies. Thus, have the larger overseas businessmen encouraged the business overseas with China and sent business overseas with their outsourcing, (unregulated for too long), which had been overlooked as a major economic issue, by the former Bush administration, as reported on several news media stations other than C-Span, just last night, November 14th, 2010. Apparently, the News has it, that smaller businessman has gotten squeezed for long enough. It is known that big business sent jobs overseas and caused American markets to constrict, here at home, while ignoring the primary Constitutional responsibility to the smaller business neighbor businessman, to allow him his *fair share* of *tax relief* and proper duties and excises levied in trade, through legislation in trade, (which is also part of the Constitution). The big business sector has limited the small business sector which is now strained in some cases according to the News updates. The smaller business sector translates as well into the Public Sector jobs arena, or influences jobs found in the Public Sector. Corporations can offer Public Sector jobs and do cater to the Private Sector where jobs have been plentiful during the Bush administration until later. Public Sector jobs became more available only in the last 18 months, predominantly, I have noted in my online research. There needs to be a bigger shift in the economy.

Cap and Trade to lower emissions and to limit costs in energy which Senator Jud Gregg, Henry Waxman and Markey proposed, was designed to increase taxes to bring to the Federal Government and give money to the Oil Industries says Charles Bass H.S. House Candidate from New Hampshire regarding the energy bill. The rich filibustered or stopped bills of oil regulation attempted, due to their long standing power, aided by the former Bush Administration. The BP issue, as well as other oil spill atrocities, makes one wonder if the amount of money left in the government is sufficient to keep SSI and the government Securities afloat, given the recent financial crisis we have just begun to recover from, as the U.S. was so very close to another Great Depression, created by the rich big business private sector, and how they did business, fostered by the former Bush Administration. The get rich incentivizing started with the Gingrich era, as remarked about by political historians, and economists, so in essence, the markets got more constricted over time and incentives provided for businesspersons to do business overseas, or outsourcing, eventually got out of hand, as did the Corporate outsourcing . How can we "invest" in business when business falls off due to outsourcing and larger business not paying its share, fails to take up the slack of putting back toward the surplus the provisions necessary for higher financial fiscal responsibility and business in this country, which allow our stability to flourish, if you will, to be in a sense "insured or cushioned" against the unknown, for others to be able to take out loans, as they have far less money or access to it?. If people are squeezed as it is, it isn't just or fair, much less common sense for the larger earners to not take up the tax burden with where the financial stability is in today's market. That seems to make sound sense. As well, benefitting employees, then locking them out, and raising their insurance premiums, makes no sense at all. Too much business not regulated has, as stated by President Obama, put America "into a ditch" already, as has been metaphorically illustrated in many political discussions. If people who have been harmed by this philosophy, oppressed by it, seek to escape the burden of the squeeze to get some relief, then it is time to do something about this model of business practice. THAT is obvious. America was built with understanding and fairness, not squeezing people to the extent that they cannot survive. Let us understand that opportunity costs usually sacrifice one product for another. If you want to sacrifice bushels of wheat for example to build war tanks, then there is a cost involved for that sacrifice, to a country or Nation. Similarly, if you have an economic curve which is shifted toward an upward curve for those who make profits, then you must consider what sacrifices need to be made to shift that curve in such a way as to stabilize the economy for the best economic outcomes for the Nation and not just some business persons who are not inclined to feel the pinch or sacrifice. One has to understand in other words that at some point, the bushels of wheat will be at a greater level of importance to the country or Nation than war tanks in that one must feed a hungry population, for example. One cannot build endless war tanks for example, nor allow endless tax breaks for the upwardly wealthy, while smaller businessmen are getting squeezed at their income levels, as a cost for opportunity expended for another sector and its profits, in an increasingly global economy. For the need of the bushels of wheat, so to speak, at some point, the economy must shift –similarly, tax relief must shift, in an increasingly populated and interdependent economy, to benefit the growing sectors of jobs at home in a country, just as those growing sectors being grown outside, off the shores of home, for example, are growing, by way of illustration. Remember, the job creation mostly took place this last business cycle in the Private Sector where most of the money has already been made, while too little job growth took place in the Public Sector, which can do harm to the economy where the economic curve has not yet shifted sufficiently for a full economic recovery, while profits and a life of comfort, greater ease and in some cases, lavish enjoyment of that lifestyle, among the wealthy, has been enjoyed, as well, has seen steady improvement in the Private sector, for years, as compared to small business, across the landscape of America in the 50 states, who are trying to catch up, if you listen to the people, the businesses, and their stories, and the stories of their employees and needs in America—as well, if you have heard those kind of life stories in the past elections and in business in general, in the global economy, then you see what is at stake. Take a look at the difference in the lifestyles to see indicators of who needs a break and who has had the break. Lifestyles can offer indications of enjoyment of life, or of burden concerning where the market is and where the current needs are, as regards the problems and lost jobs due to outsourcing as a consequence of providing profits for managers who chose a different management strategy, and this factor too, once again stated, is what has slowed growth in some sectors, or squeezed sectors of business, due to the benefitting of one sector over another, which is a common principle of economics and growth statistics, or *opportunity costs* in any given economy and cycles of an economy concerning overall Gross Domestic Product and the Gross National Product of a Nation, or, what is produced in a Nation at home, versus what is produced in the Nation as a whole, regarding regulations in business, at home and in foreign trade, which require being properly regulated for good business practice for best growth, executed over time, in each sector as economics is about maintaining a sound and delicate balance.